# Mandalas

Capturing the essence of individuals, coloring pages featuring portraits provide a canvas to express emotions and explore the depth of human expression, allowing colorists to create personal connections and artistic interpretations.

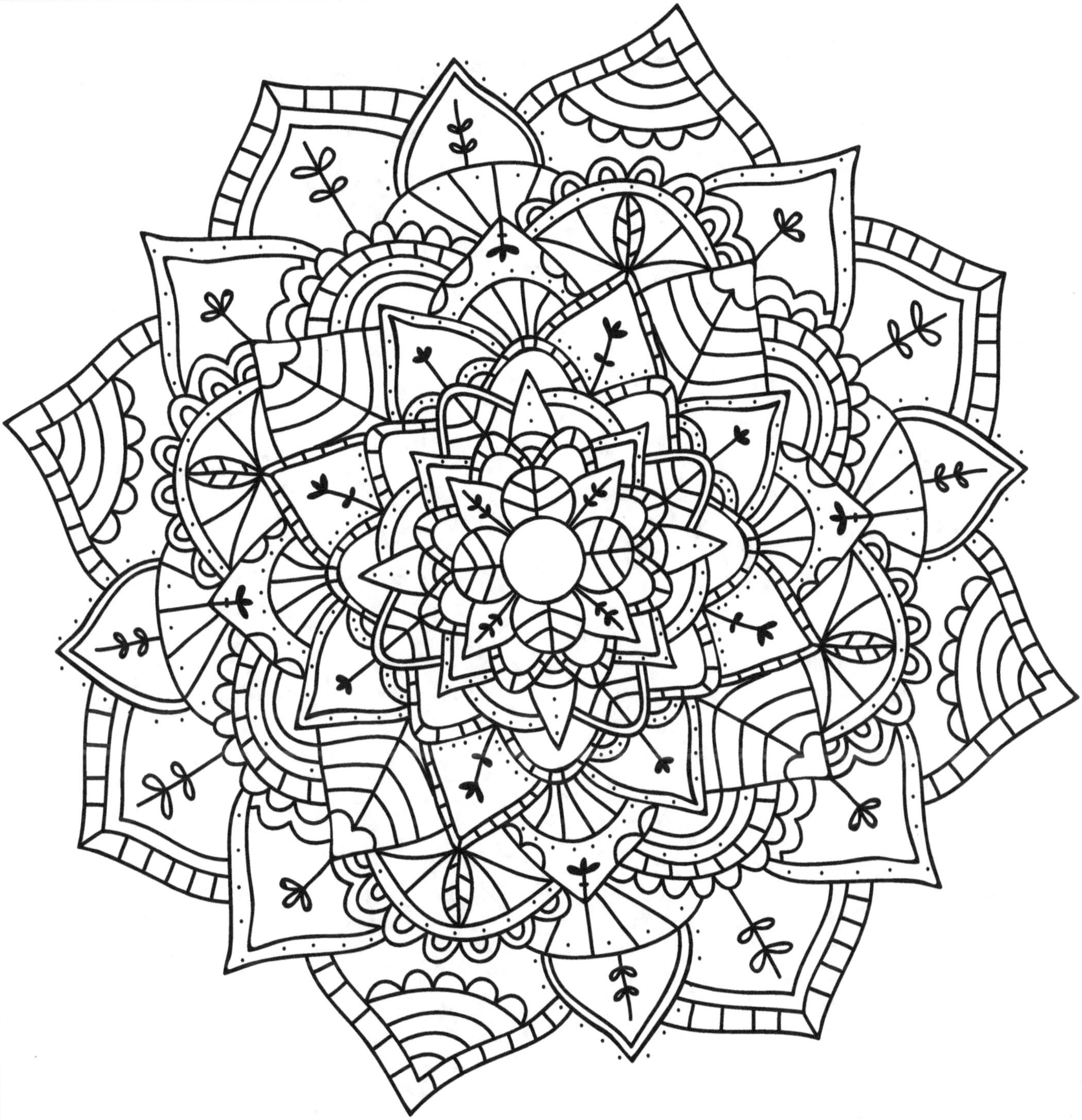

Imagine walking along a winding forest path, surrounded by the peacefulness of nature, as it leads you to a hidden gem—Buddha temple nestled amidst the trees. The soothing sound of a nearby stream whispers a calming melody, adding to the harmony of the surroundings. The scent of moss and earth fills the air, grounding you in the present moment. As you approach the temple, the soft chiming of wind chimes greets your ears, inviting you to enter this sacred space of peace and contemplation. Here, amidst the ancient trees and the timeless wisdom embodied by the Buddha statue.

01

# Zen Doodles

Free-flowing pen strokes intertwine, resulting in intricate and meditative doodles, inviting individuals to find serenity and unleash their creativity.

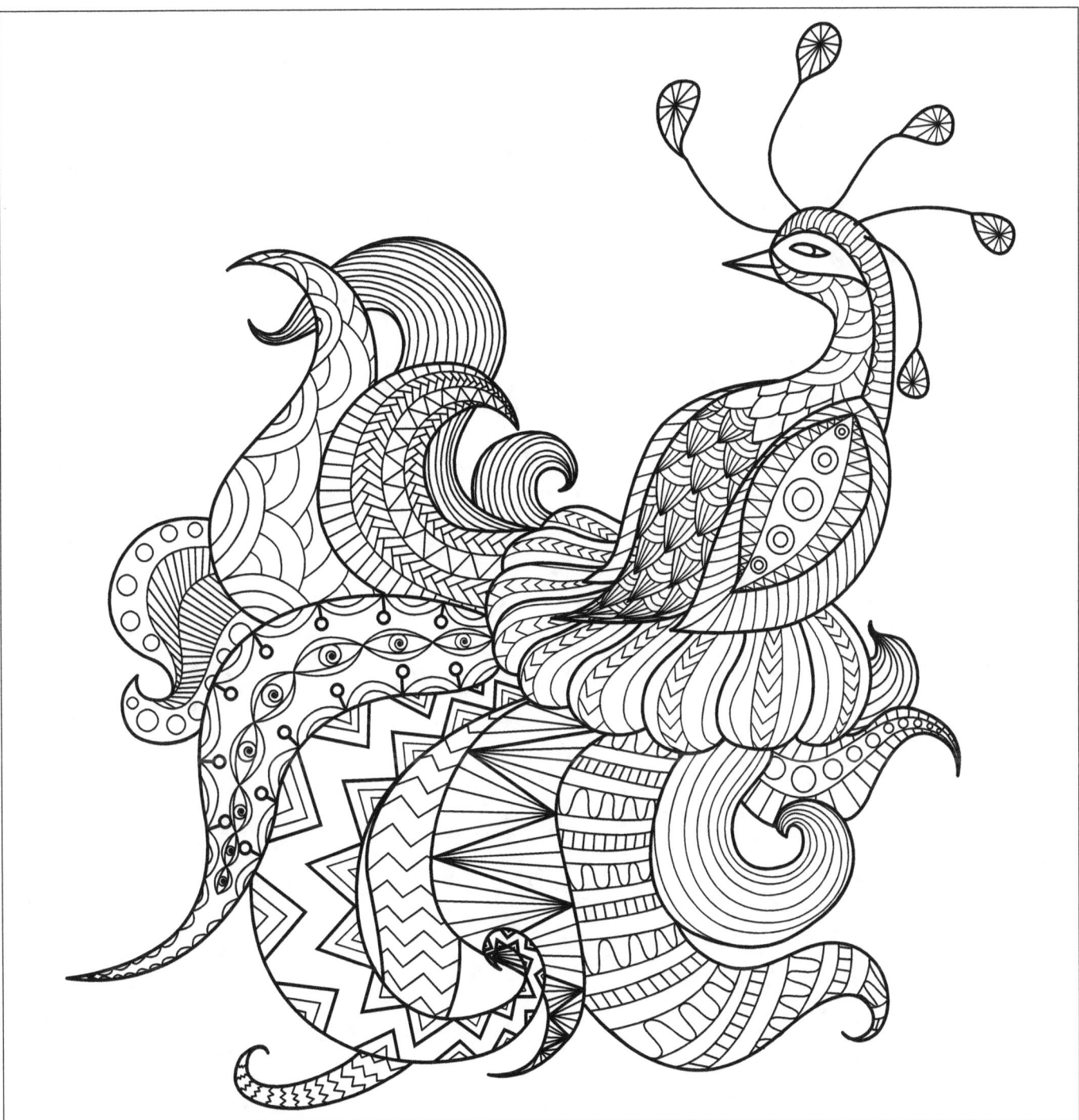

Picture yourself on a peaceful beach. The soft wind rustles through the palm trees, creating a gentle whisper. The waves gracefully glide onto the shore, their rhythmic motion lulling you into a state of calm. You recline in a cozy hammock, swaying gently back and forth, embraced by a sense of harmony. The gentle symphony of nature's sounds harmonizes with your heartbeat, creating a soothing rhythm that lulls you into a state of deep relaxation. The serene ambiance and the soothing sounds of nature bring a deep feeling of peace and relaxation.

02

# Zentangles

Delicate ink lines meticulously interlace, forming elaborate patterns that calm the mind and foster focus, creating a therapeutic experience of art and self-expression.

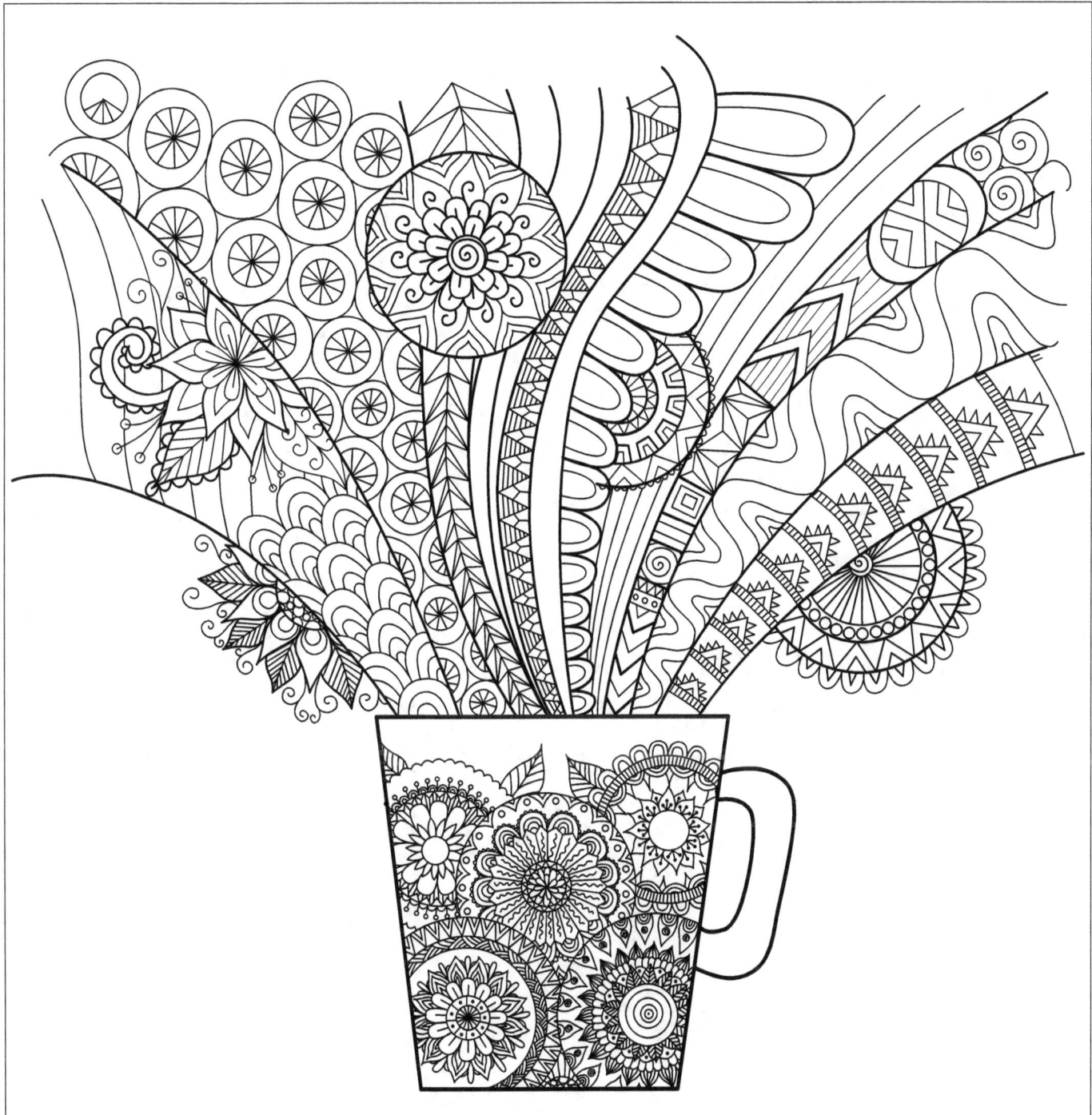

In a serene garden, everything feels calm and peaceful. The thoughtfully arranged elements create a soothing atmosphere. As you sit among the lush greenery, you take in the delightful scent of flowers. When you close your eyes, you can hear the gentle sounds of nature: leaves softly rustling and birds softly singing. In this peaceful space, worries fade away, leaving behind a sense of tranquility. You find comfort and joy in the simplicity of the moment, appreciating the beauty of the garden surrounding you.

**03**

# Inspirational Quotes

Meaningful words of encouragement seamlessly blend with artistic illustrations, igniting motivation and positivity, uplifting spirits and enhancing the coloring experience.

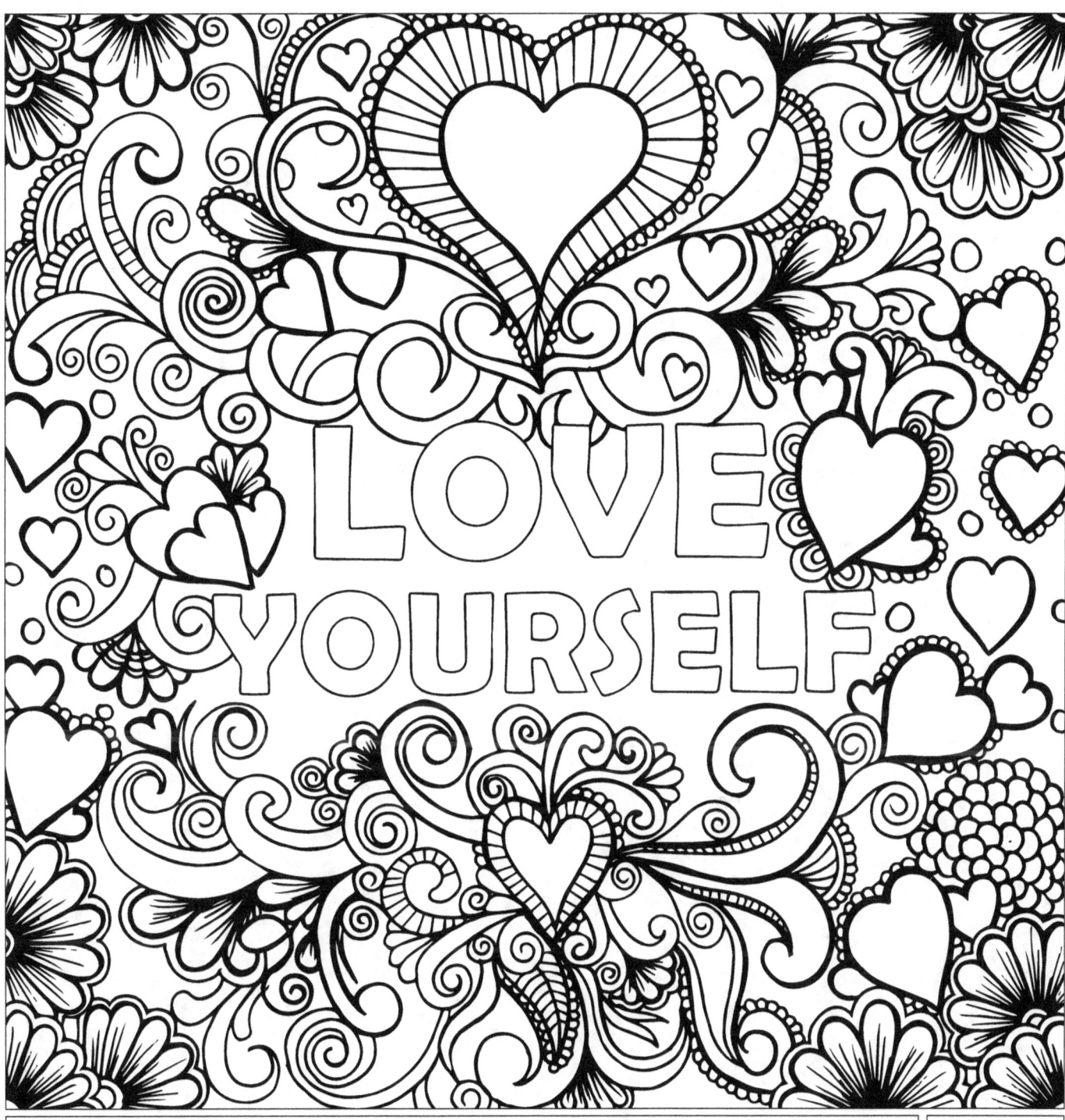

On the mountaintop, a sense of calmness fills the air. The tall peaks stand proudly, reaching towards the sky. The view is awe-inspiring, with hills and lakes stretching as far as the eye can see. The air is fresh and invigorating, rejuvenating your every breath. The quiet surroundings bring a deep sense of peace, occasionally interrupted by the delightful songs of birds and the distant sound of flowing water. As you make your way down, carry the memory of this peaceful moment and the reminder to find balance in life's journey.

**04**

# Fantasy Worlds

Vibrant hues breathe life into imaginary realms, transcending reality, and enabling colorists to embark on enchanting journeys where imagination knows no bounds.

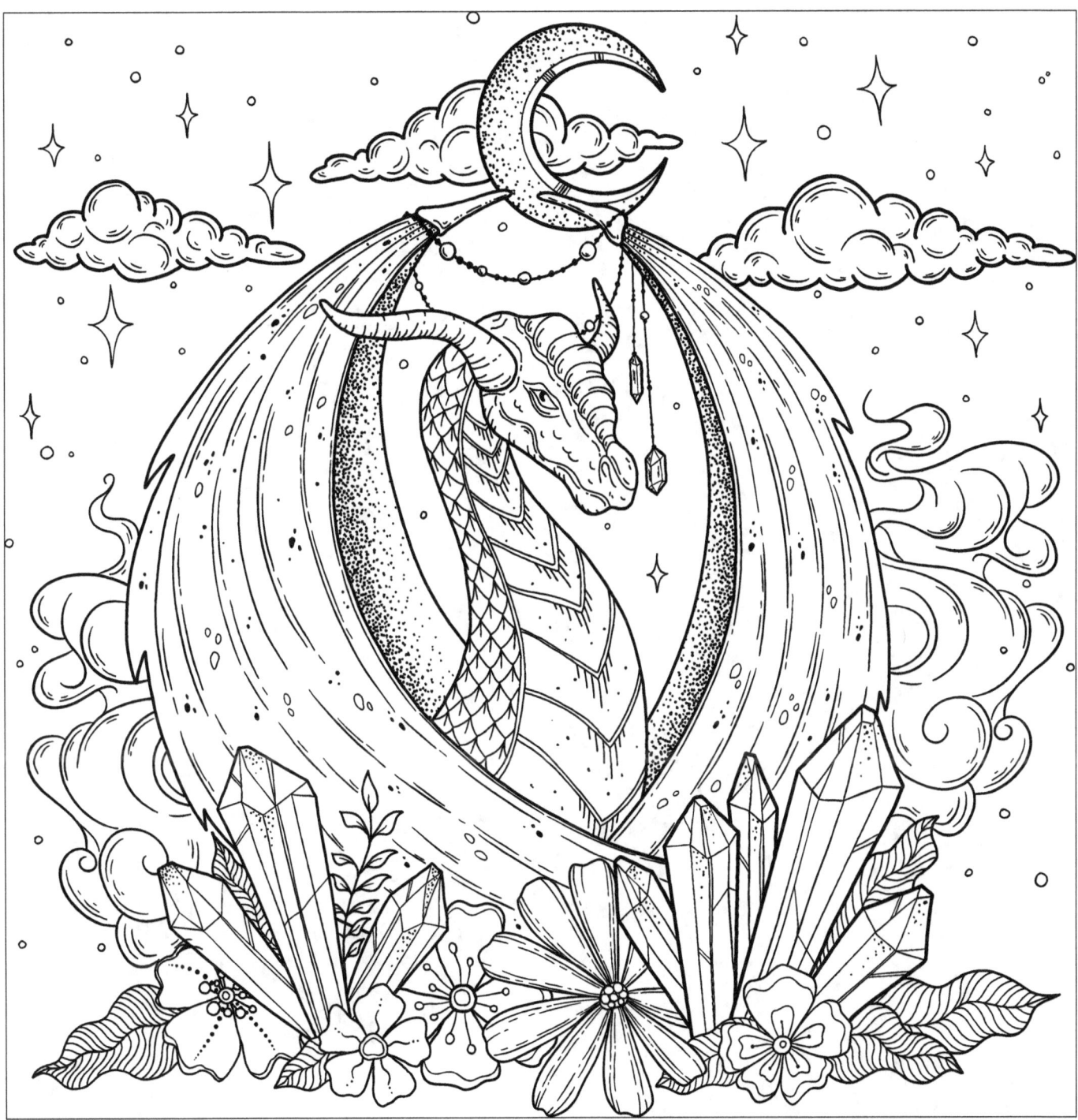

Picture yourself at a peaceful lakeside, where a sense of calmness envelops you. The water is still and mirrors the beauty of nature. As you sit by the shore, gentle ripples create a soothing effect. You can hear the soft sounds of water gently lapping against the shore and birds singing their sweet melodies. As you gaze at your reflection on the glassy water, a feeling of inner serenity washes over you. As you leave the lakeside, carry this peacefulness with you, reminding yourself of the importance of stillness and self-reflection.

**05**

# Steampunk

Steampunk art emerged as a captivating fusion of Victorian aesthetics and steam-powered technology, whisking us away to a fantastical realm of gears, goggles, and imaginative contraptions.

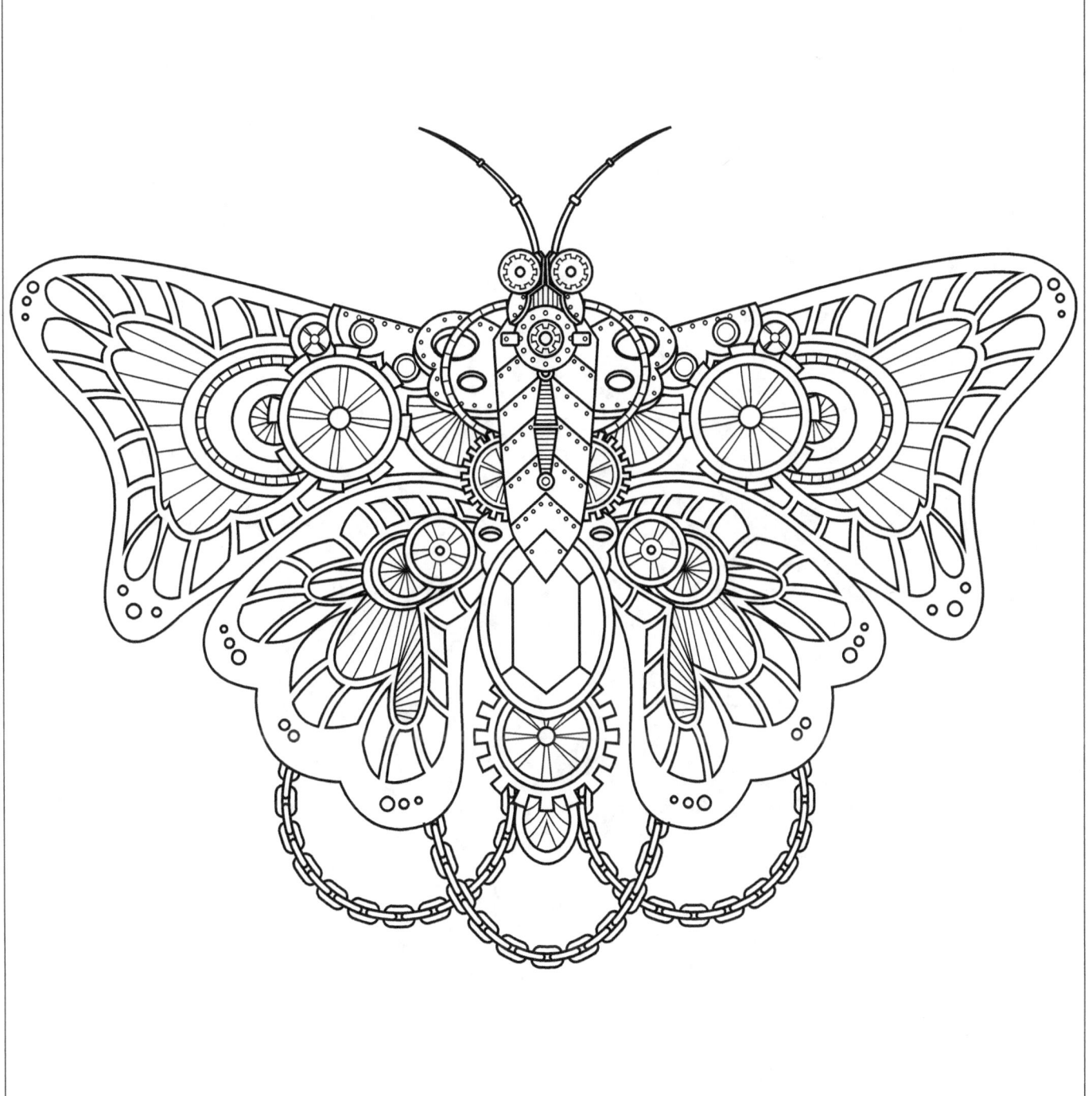

Picture a beautiful meadow at dawn. Find a comfortable spot among the tall grass and wildflowers. Close your eyes and take a deep breath, feeling the cool morning air on your skin. Listen to the sounds of nature awakening around you - birds singing, leaves gently rustling. Feel connected to the earth beneath you, grounding yourself in the present moment. Notice the soft rays of sunlight filtering through the trees, casting a warm glow over the meadow. Feel the gentle texture of the grass against your fingertips. Embrace the peacefulness of this moment and carry it with you.

06

# Day of the Dead

It combines indigenous Mesoamerican traditions and Catholic influences to create a vibrant celebration honoring departed loved ones, with colorful altars, sugar skulls, and joyful remembrance.

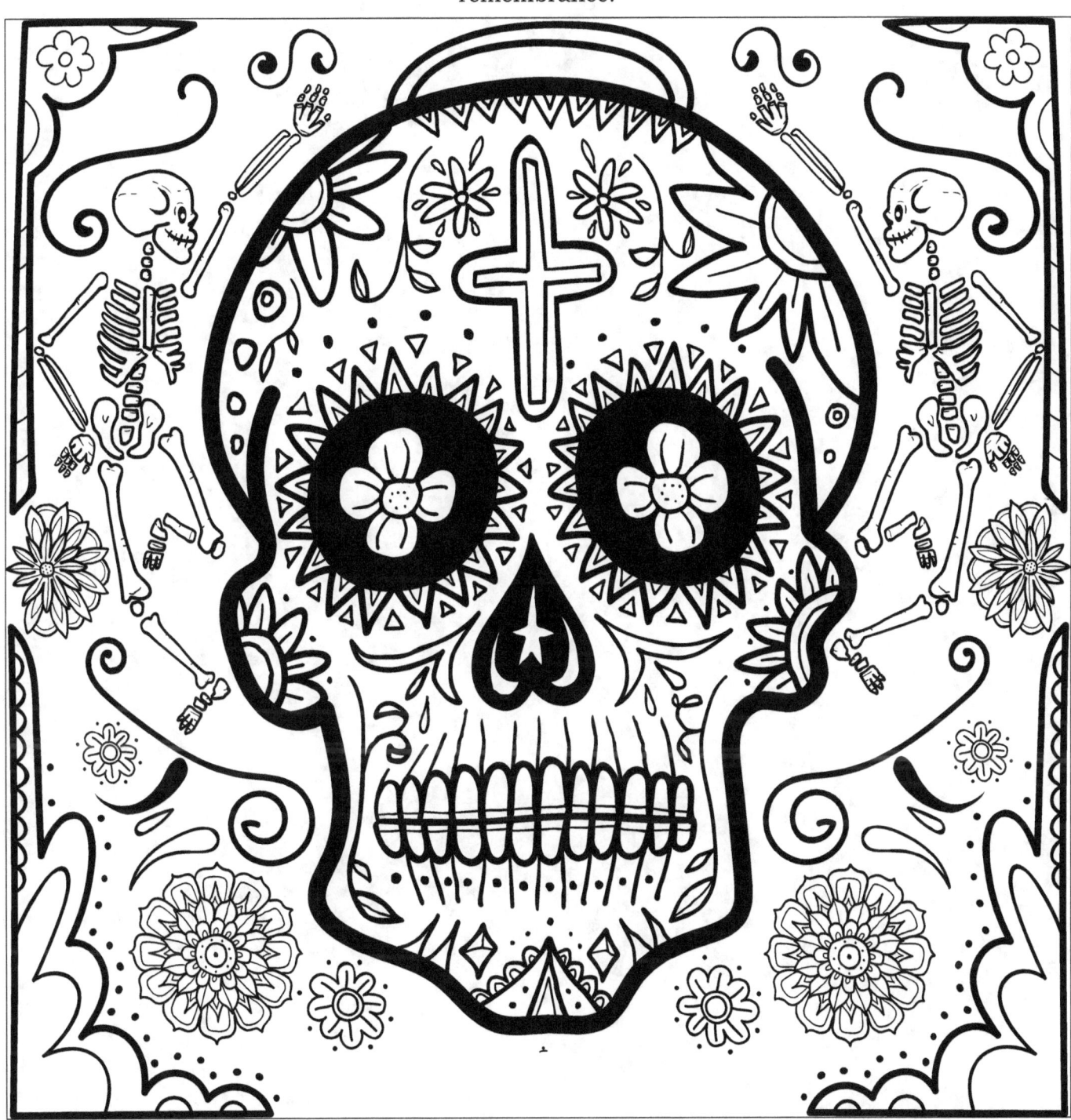

Imagine being in a candlelit meditation retreat. Find a comfortable spot and close your eyes. Focus on the soft glow of the flickering candles, creating a peaceful atmosphere. Breathe in the calming energy and exhale any tension. Let the warmth of the candlelight soothe your senses. Allow your thoughts to come and go without judgment. Embrace the stillness and be present in the moment. When you're ready, slowly open your eyes, feeling refreshed and carrying the serene feeling with you.

07

# Art Nouveau

A flourishing artistic movement originating in the late 19th century, characterized by the harmonious fusion of human forms and organic elements now celebrated through coloring and artistic expression.

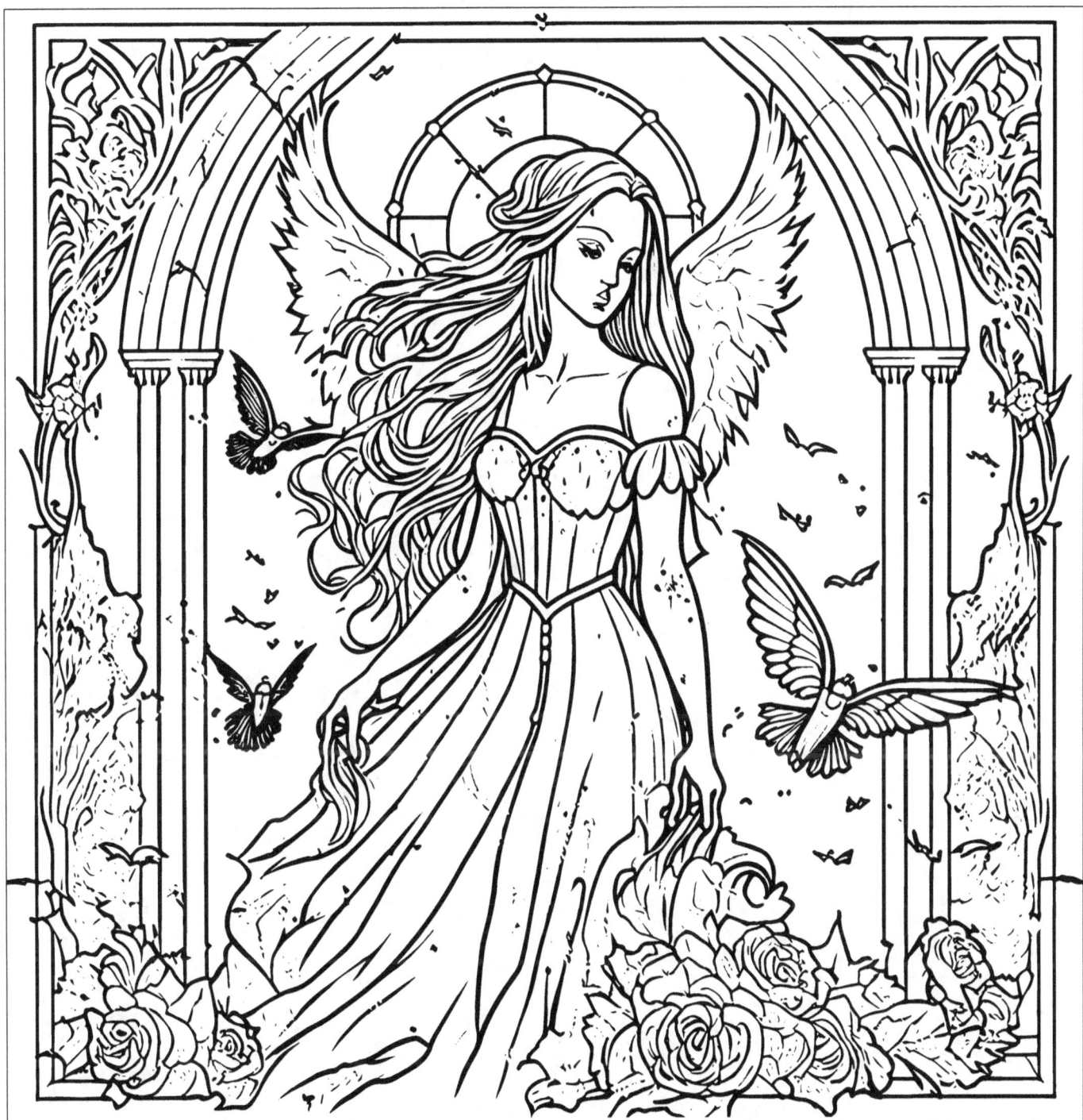

Imagine the gentle sound of rain falling. Picture yourself in a cozy spot, listening to the soft patter of raindrops on the window. The rhythmic sound brings a feeling of calmness. Close your eyes and breathe in the fresh smell of rain. Feel the peace as each drop lands, washing away any worries. Relax under a warm blanket, enjoying the soothing atmosphere. As the rain continues, find comfort and renewal in its gentle embrace. When you open your eyes, carry the serene feeling of the rain with you, remembering to seek moments of peace and relaxation.

08

# Kaleidoscopic Designs

Patterns reminiscent of a mesmerizing kaleidoscope unfold, capturing attention and evoking wonder, making them popular for coloring and relaxation.

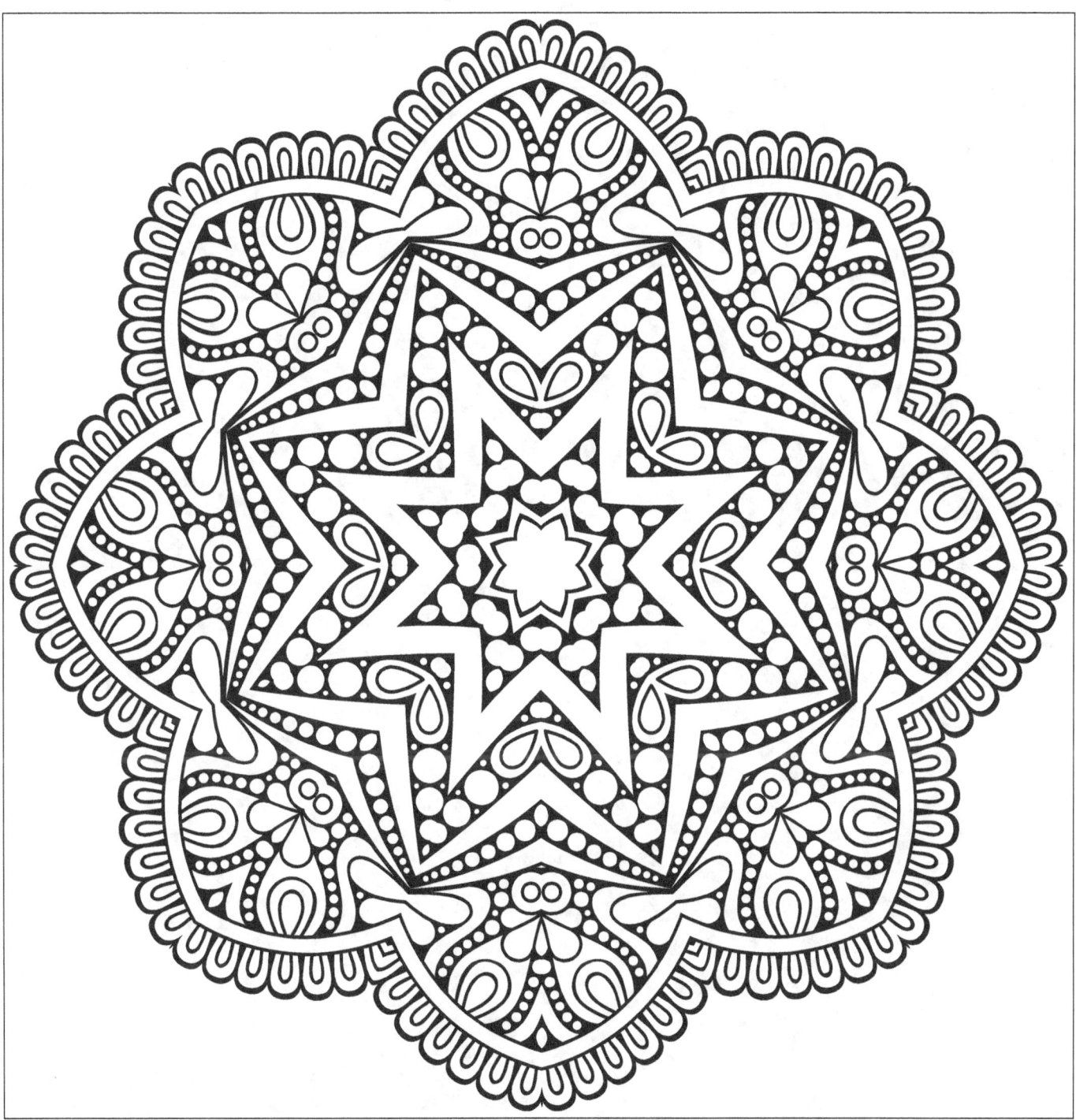

Imagine floating on fluffy clouds, feeling weightless. Picture yourself lying down and gently drifting through the sky. The clouds beneath you are soft and comforting. Look up and see the clouds passing by, each with its own unique shape. Listen to the quietness around you, allowing it to bring a sense of calm. Feel a lightness and freedom as you float, as if being carried by the clouds themselves. Let your mind wander and dream as you connect with your inner self. As you slowly descend, hold on to the feeling of floating on clouds.

**09**

# Celestial Themes

Stars, moons, and galaxies converge in celestial designs, captivating the imagination and allowing individuals to explore cosmic realms through coloring and artistic expression.

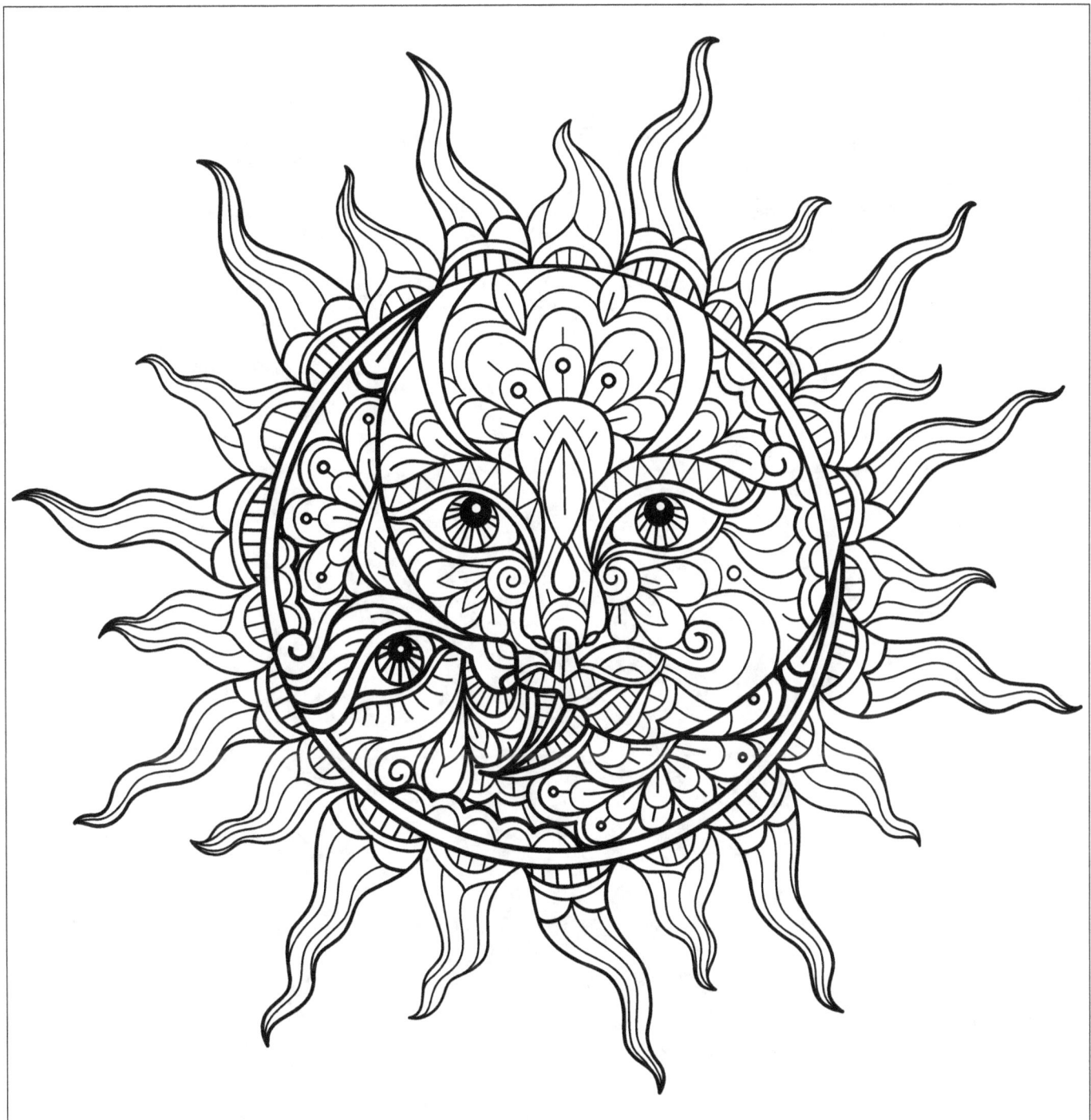

Imagine sitting on a mountain peak at sunrise. Close your eyes and feel the warm sun on your face. Take deep breaths of fresh air. As the sunrise unfolds, take a few more moments to enjoy the beauty of the colors and the awakening nature around you. Relax your mind as you enjoy the peacefulness of the mountain. As the sun rises, imagine its gentle light filling you with calmness. Focus on your breath and take in the beauty of the surroundings. When you open your eyes, carry the peaceful feeling with you throughout your day.

**10**

# Tattoo Art

Coloring books offer an edgy experience to explore intricate tattoo designs without the permanence of real ink.

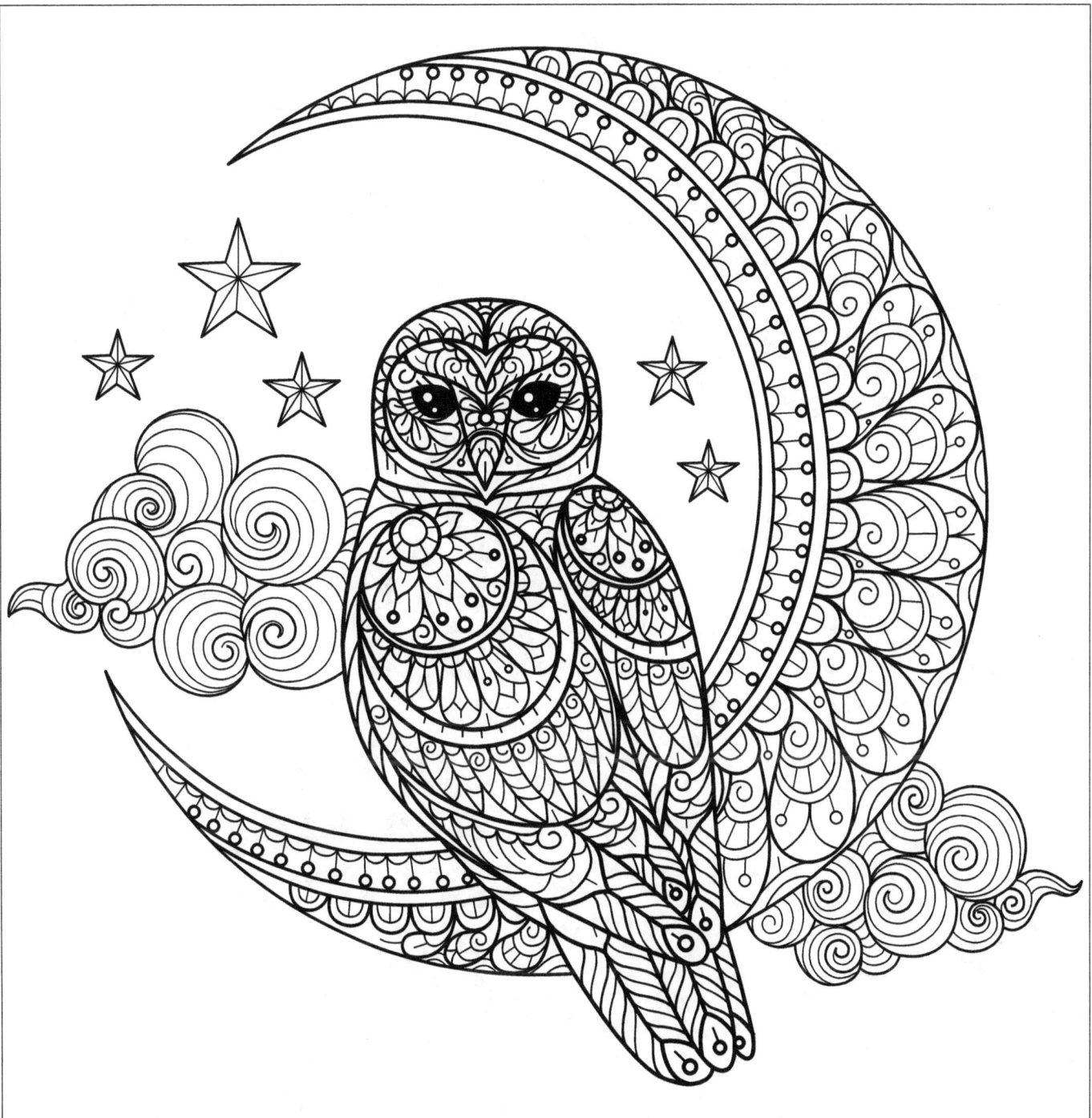

Sit by a babbling brook in a lush forest. Take a deep breath and listen to the gentle flow of water. Inhale deeply, feeling the crisp forest air fill your lungs. Exhale slowly, releasing any stress or worries. Focus on the soothing sound of the brook and the rustling of leaves overhead. Feel a sense of calmness and connection with nature envelop you. Take a moment to notice the sunlight filtering through the trees, creating a play of light and shadow. Open your eyes, carrying this peacefulness and the serene beauty of the forest with you.

**11**

# Architecture

Coloring pages bring grand structures to life, allowing enthusiasts to appreciate the beauty of architecture in a therapeutic and creative way.

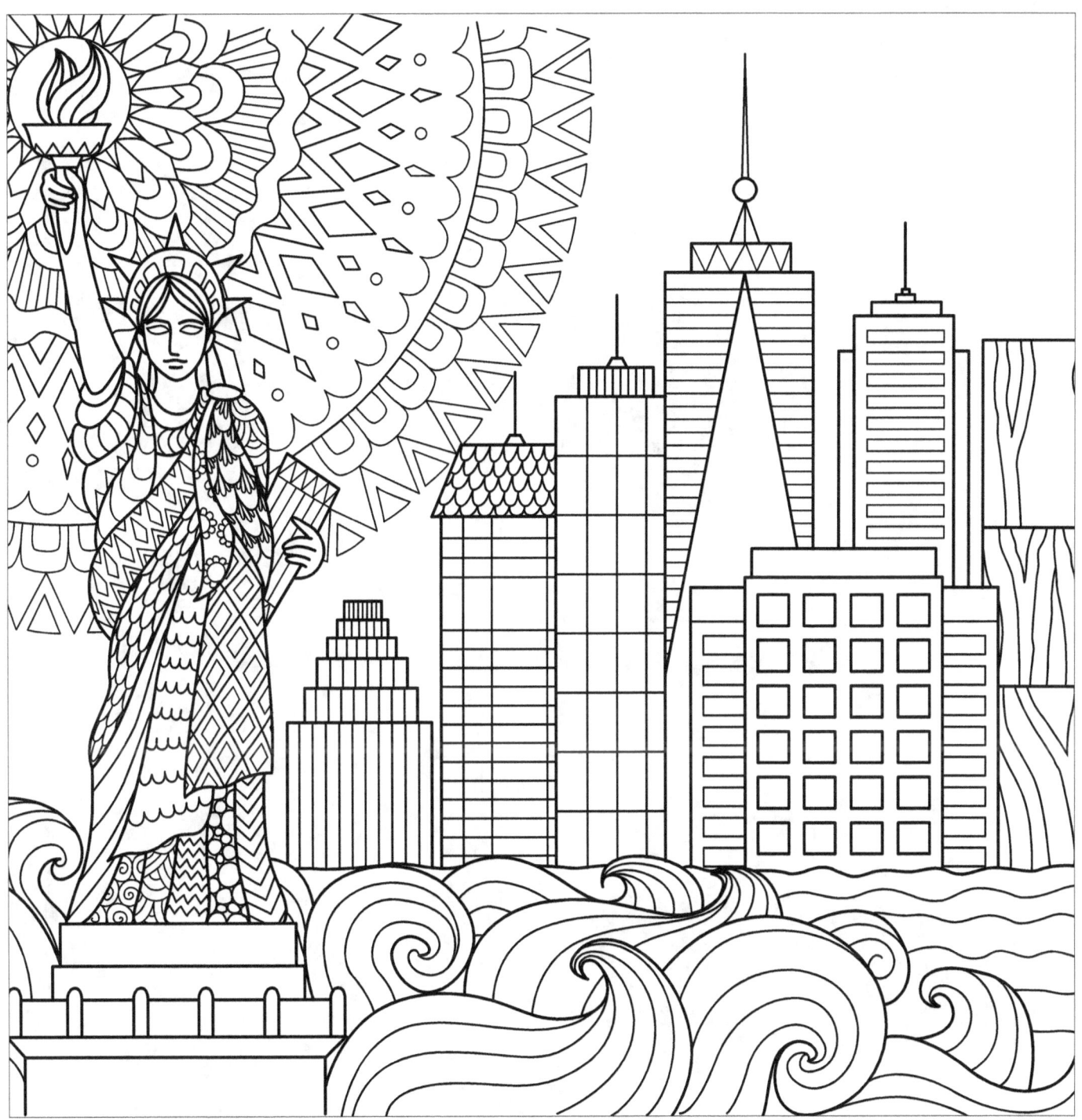

Imagine standing by a magnificent waterfall. Close your eyes and listen to the mesmerizing sounds of the water crashing and splashing. Feel the cool mist on your face, refreshing and invigorating. Take deep breaths of the crisp, pure air, filling your lungs with nature's essence. The captivating sounds of the waterfall and the surrounding wildlife create a harmonious symphony. Allow the natural melody to calm your mind and uplift your spirit. When you open your eyes, carry the peaceful energy of the waterfall with you, reminding yourself to find beauty and serenity in the world around you.

12

# Vintage Illustrations

Evoking nostalgia, vintage illustrations from the past bring forth a sense of history and charm, as exemplified by a collector stumbling upon a treasured antique print.

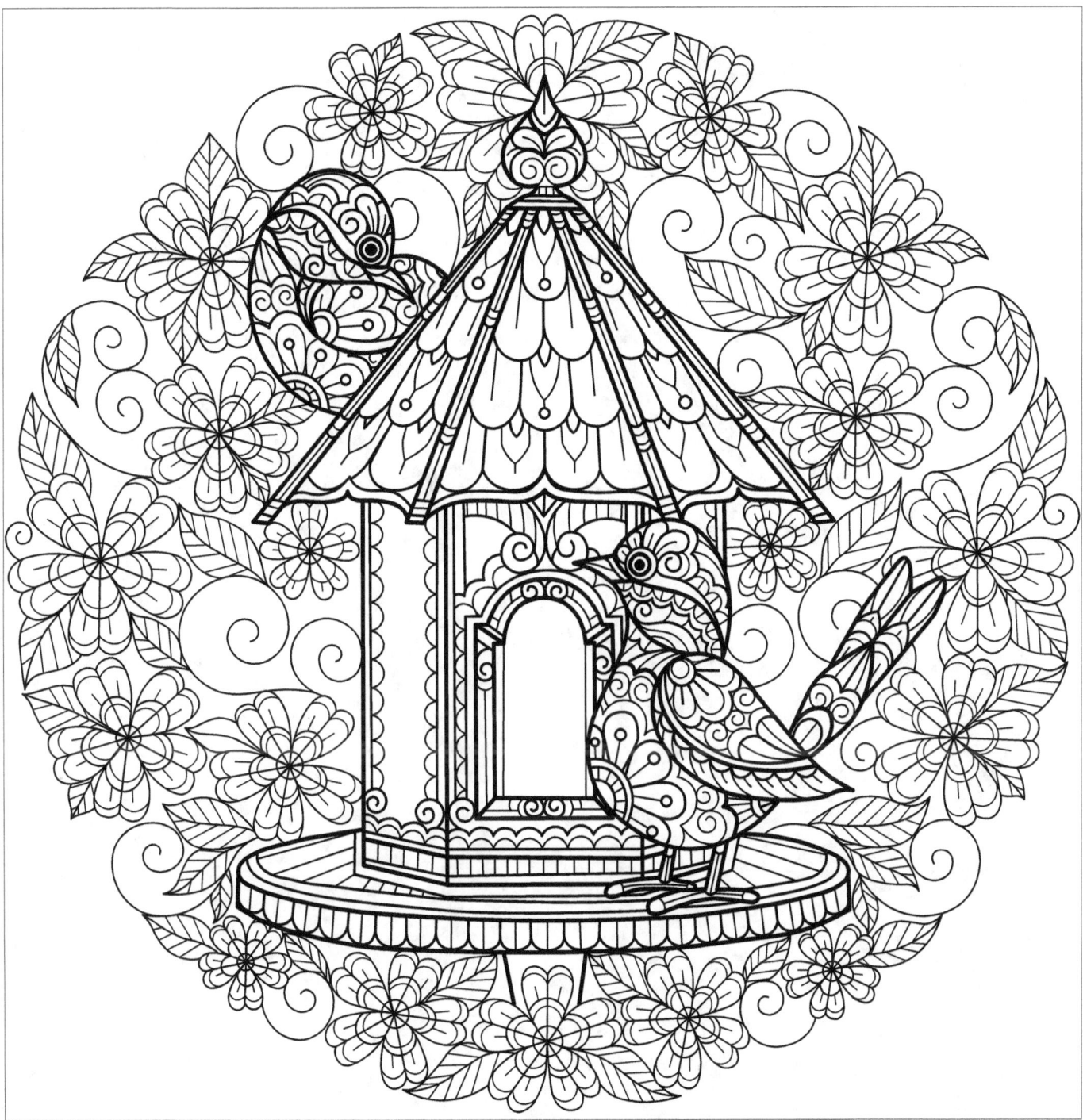

Picture yourself sitting by a calm river. Listen to the gentle flow of the water, soothing and peaceful. Breathe in the fresh scent of nature around you. Let go of any stress as you immerse yourself in this serene moment. Observe the sunlight dancing on the water's surface. Take a moment to dip your hand into the river and feel the coolness of the water against your skin. Carry the serenity of the river's flow with you as a reminder to find peace in everyday moments.

13

# Travel Destinations

Capturing the essence of wanderlust, landscapes transport enthusiasts to far-off places, allowing them to explore and reimagine their favorite travel destinations through vibrant colors.

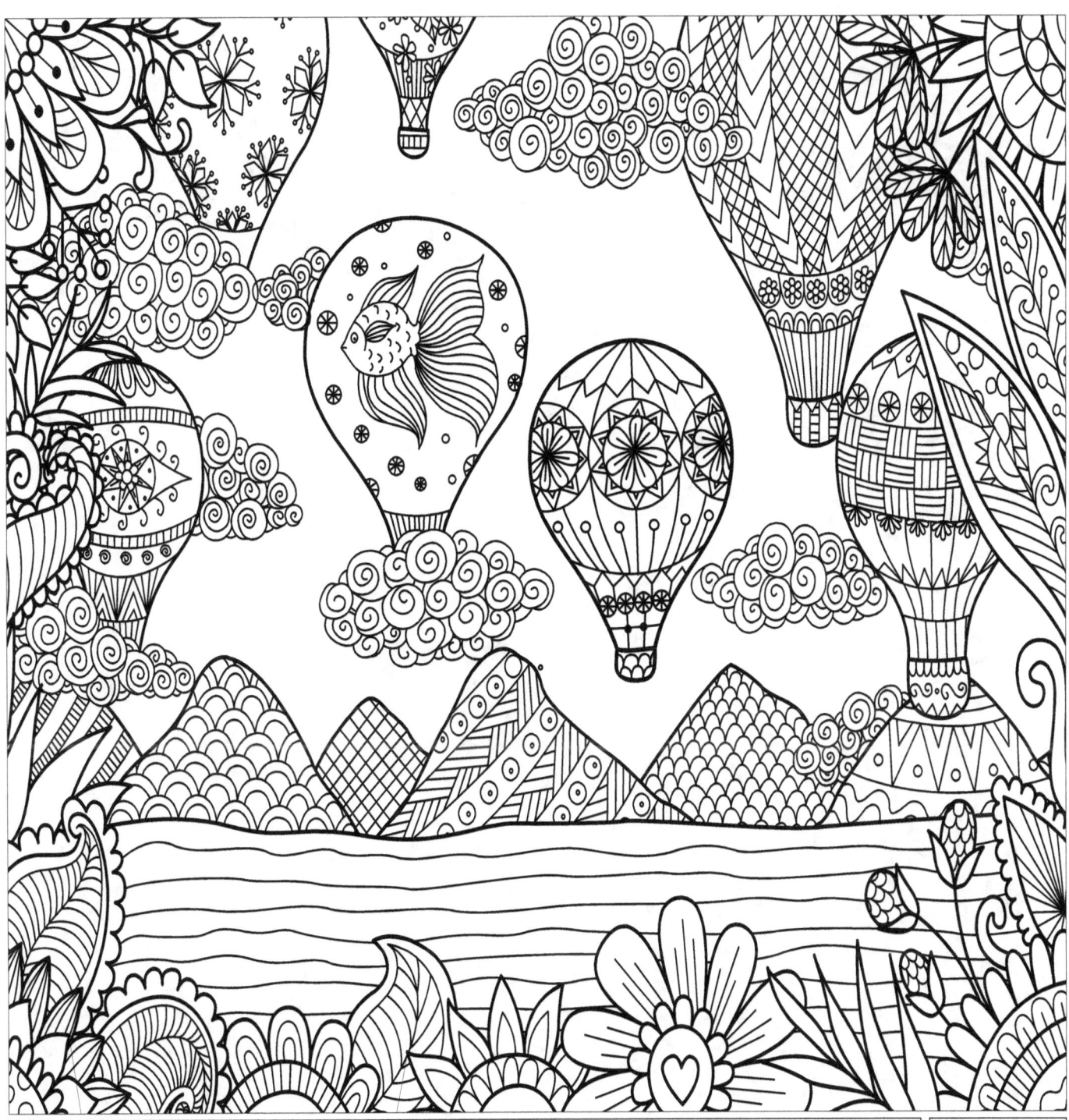

Picture yourself on a small moonlit terrace, high above the city. Feel the soft glow of the moon and take a deep breath. Let go of any worries and embrace the calmness and stillness of the night, even amidst the faint sound of late-night traffic in the distance. Listen to the distant waves crashing on the nearby shore, adding a soothing rhythm to the peaceful ambiance. Relax and enjoy the serenity of this moment, knowing that you have found a quiet sanctuary under the moonlight.

**14**

# Botanical Illustrations

Intricate plants and flowers showcase the beauty of nature, reminiscent of a botanical artist meticulously capturing the essence of each petal and leaf.

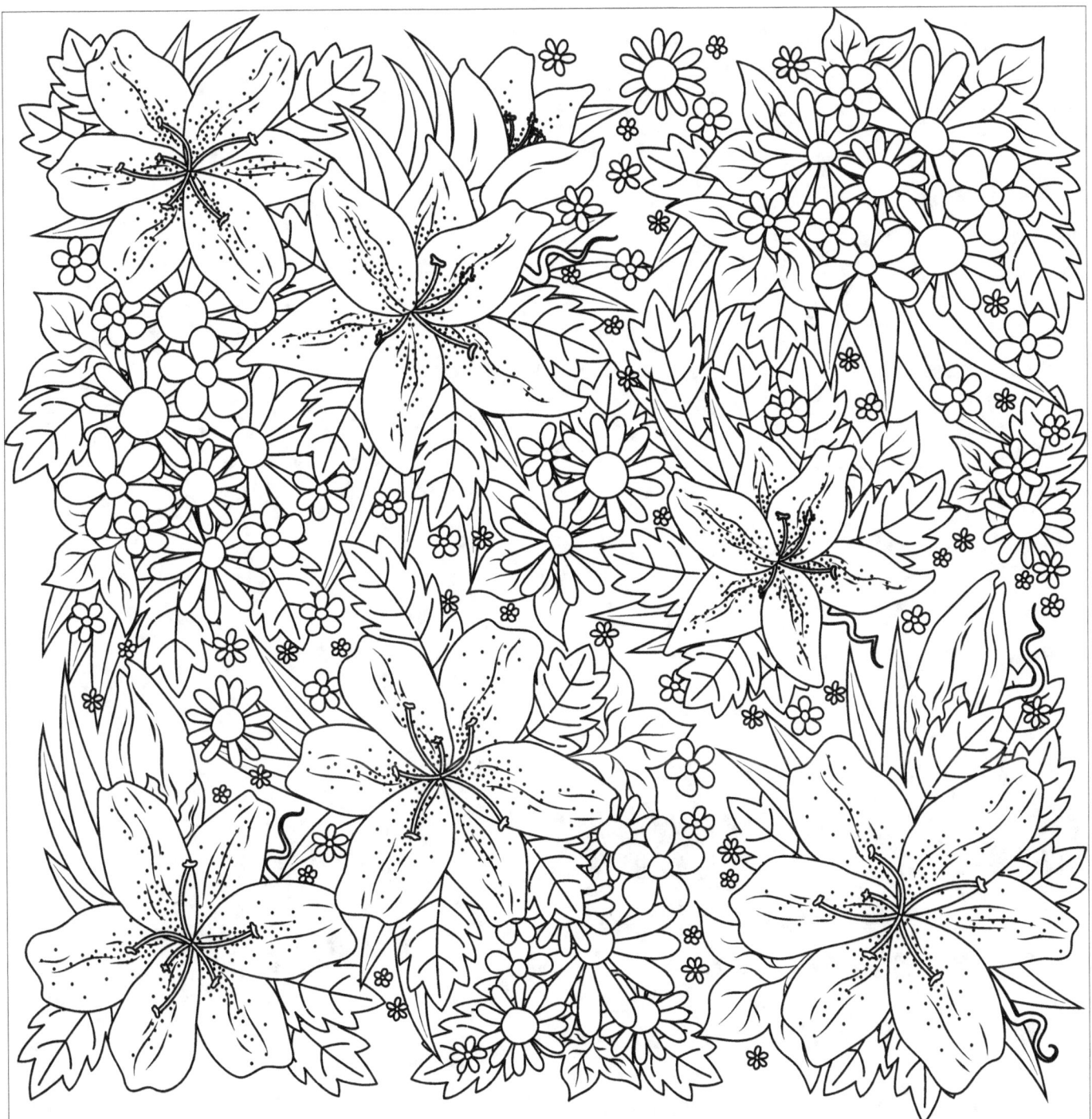

Picture a serene garden. Close your eyes and breathe in the fragrant air, filled with the sweet scent of blooming flowers. Feel the soft grass beneath your feet as you walk along the winding paths, shaded by towering trees. Listen to the birdsong and the gentle trickle of a nearby fountain, creating a harmonious symphony of nature. Find a cozy spot to sit and take in the peaceful beauty, surrounded by colorful blooms and fluttering butterflies. Embrace the calm and serenity of this garden, carrying it with you wherever you go.

**15**

# Nature Scenes

Immersed in the tranquility of natural settings, coloring pages depicting serene forests, majestic mountains, and calm lakes provide a therapeutic escape.

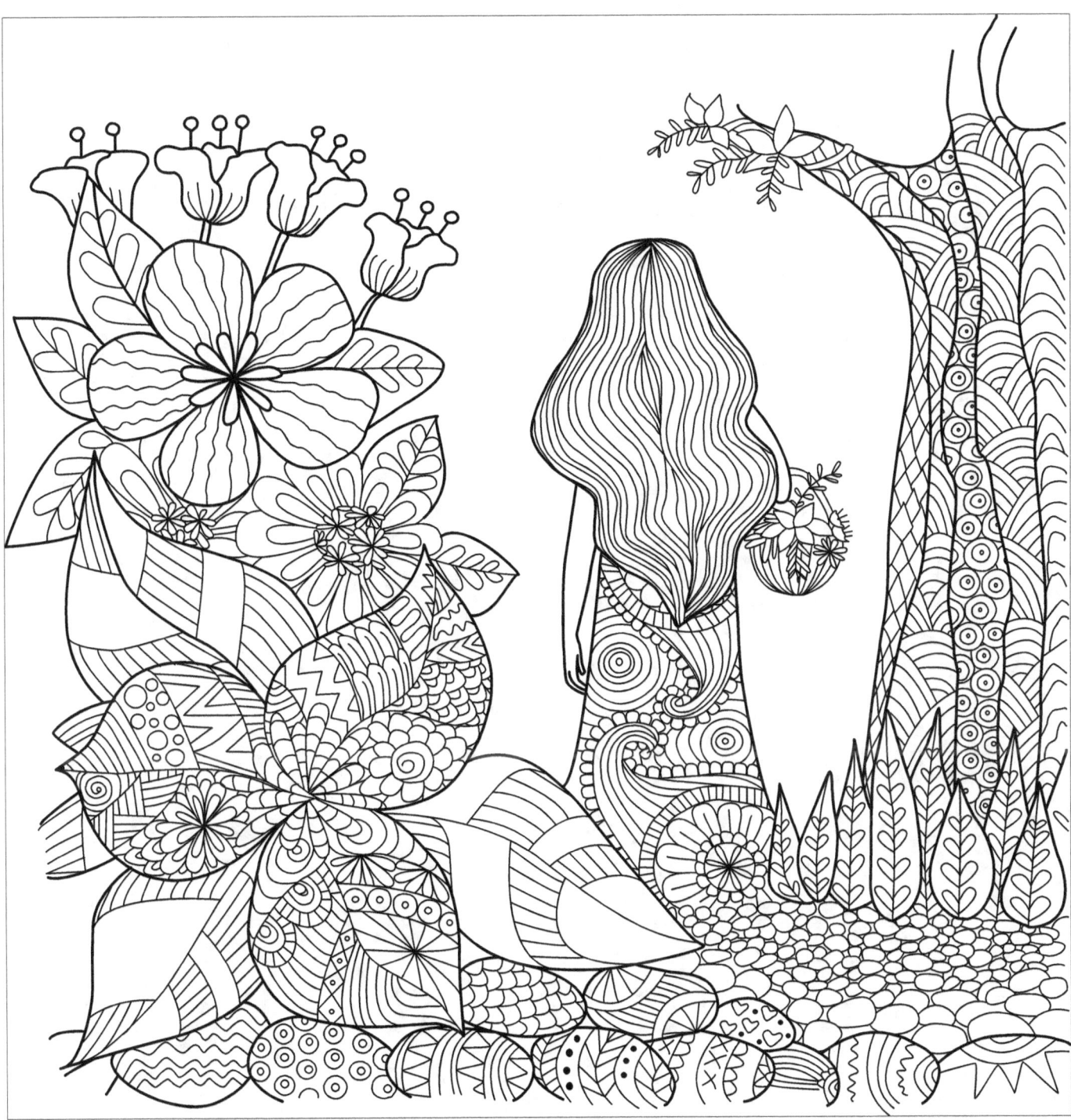

Imagine taking a mindful walk in nature. Feel the ground beneath your feet and the sun on your skin. Picture colorful flowers, swaying trees, and a peaceful atmosphere. Listen to the rustling leaves, the bird's song, and the gentle wind. Breathe in the fresh scents of flowers and earth. Let go of worries and be present in the moment. Notice the intricate details of nature. Imagine a calm mind, free of judgment. As your walk ends, carry nature's serenity with you, finding peace in your day.

**16**

# Animals

From playful kittens to majestic elephant, capture the diversity and beauty of the animal kingdom, allowing colorists to bring their favorite creatures to life with their chosen colors.

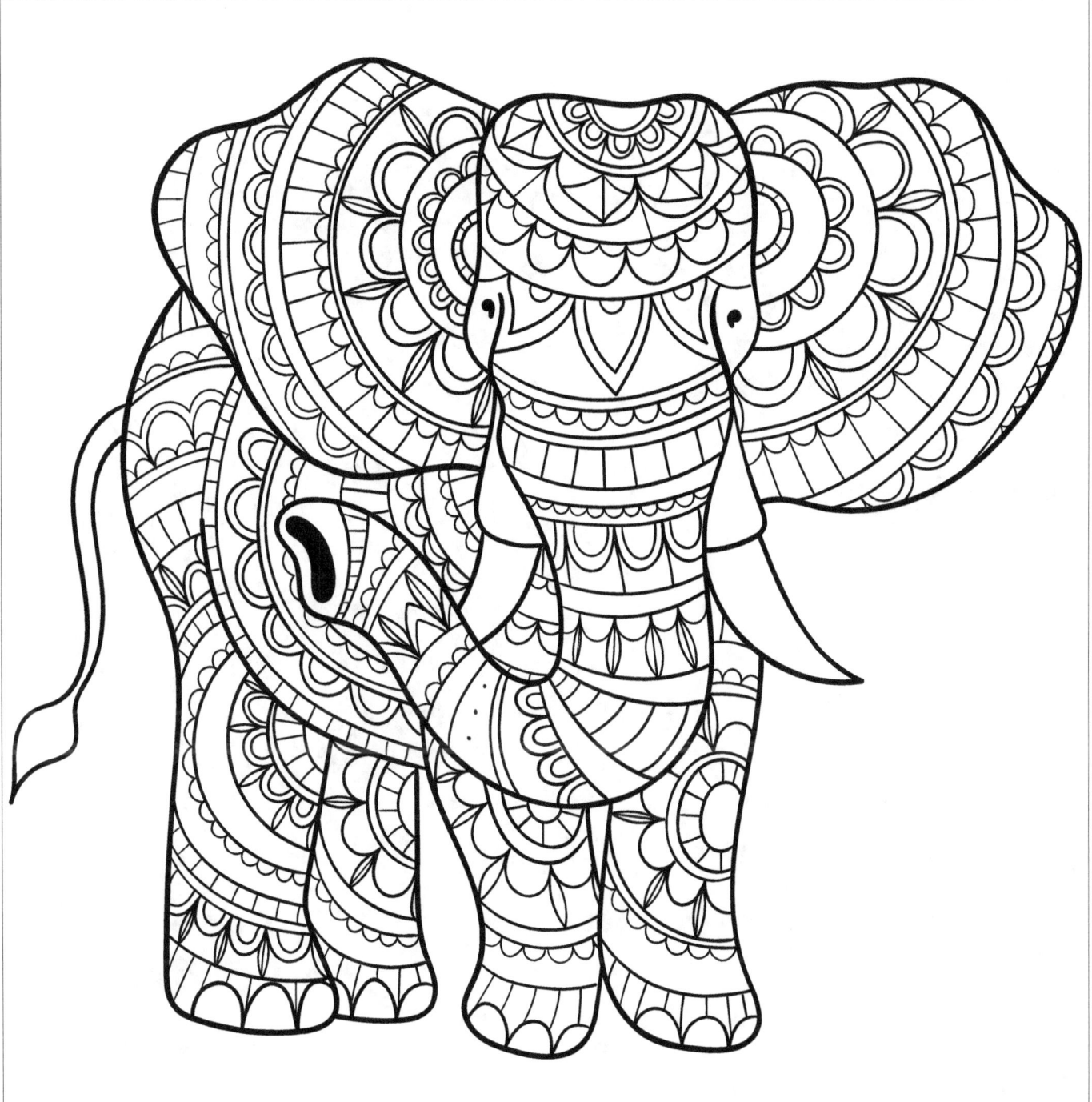

Imagine the soothing sounds of Tibetan singing bowls filling the air, creating a gentle and melodic harmony. Feel the vibrations of the bowls resonating through your body, releasing tension and promoting deep relaxation. Let the healing tones wash over you, transporting you to a place of inner peace. Stay in this moment, allowing the calming sounds to nurture your well-being and restore balance to your mind and body. When you're ready, slowly open your eyes, feeling refreshed and rejuvenated, ready to embrace the serenity that surrounds you.

17

# Abstract Art

Born out of a desire to break free from representational constraints, it emerged as a form of expression, inviting interpretation and emotional connection.

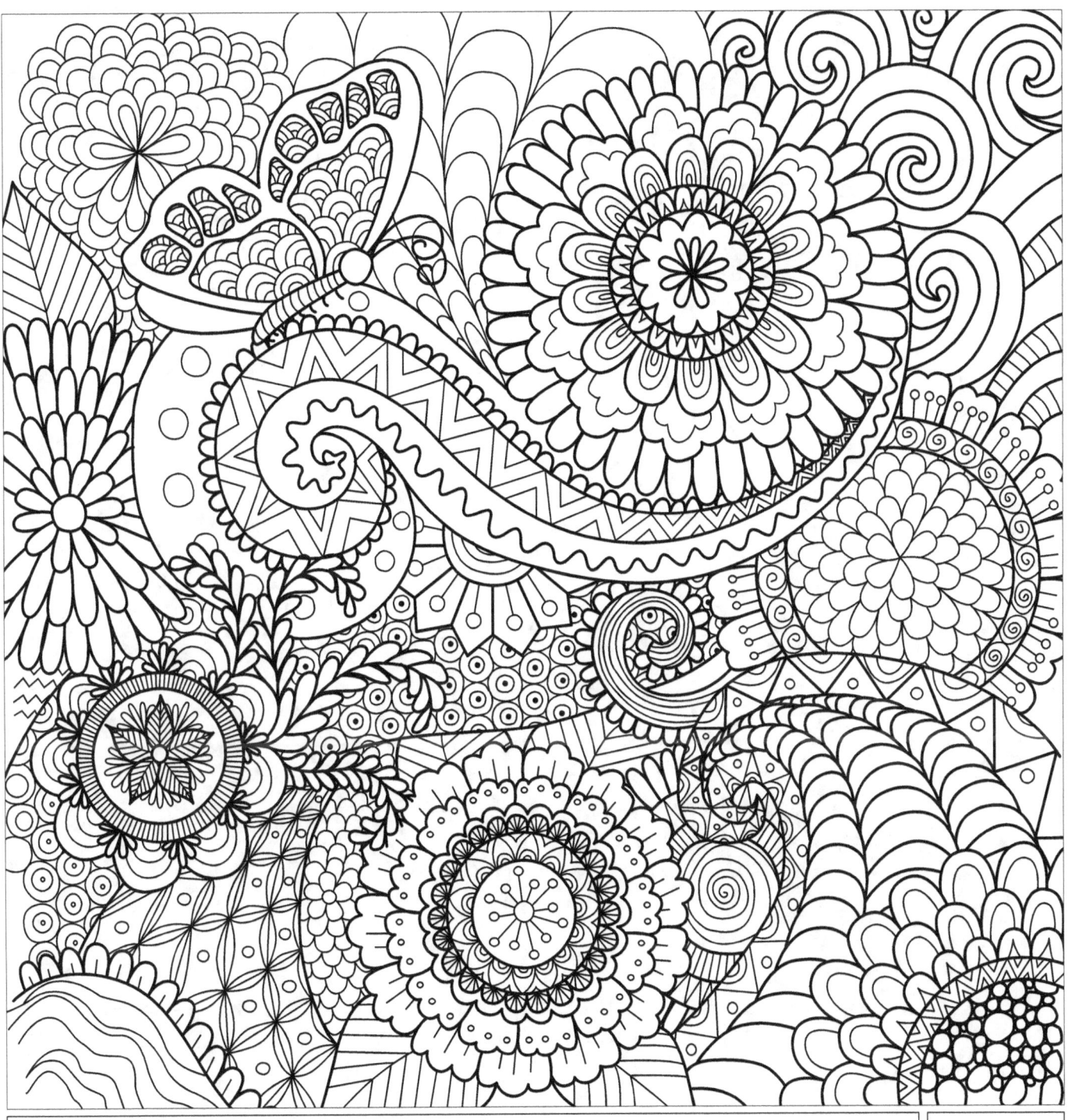

Find a comfortable position and close your eyes. Take a deep breath and bring your attention to your body. Start with your feet and notice any sensations or tension. With each exhale, release any tightness or discomfort. Move your focus up to your legs, hips, and abdomen. Let go of any tension as you breathe out. Continue to scan your body, releasing tension from your chest, shoulders, arms, and hands. Relax your neck, jaw, and face. When you're ready, gently open your eyes and carry this sense of relaxation with you.

**18**

# Geometric Patterns

Derived from mathematical principles, geometric patterns showcase the beauty of symmetry and precision and the exploration of geometric aesthetics.

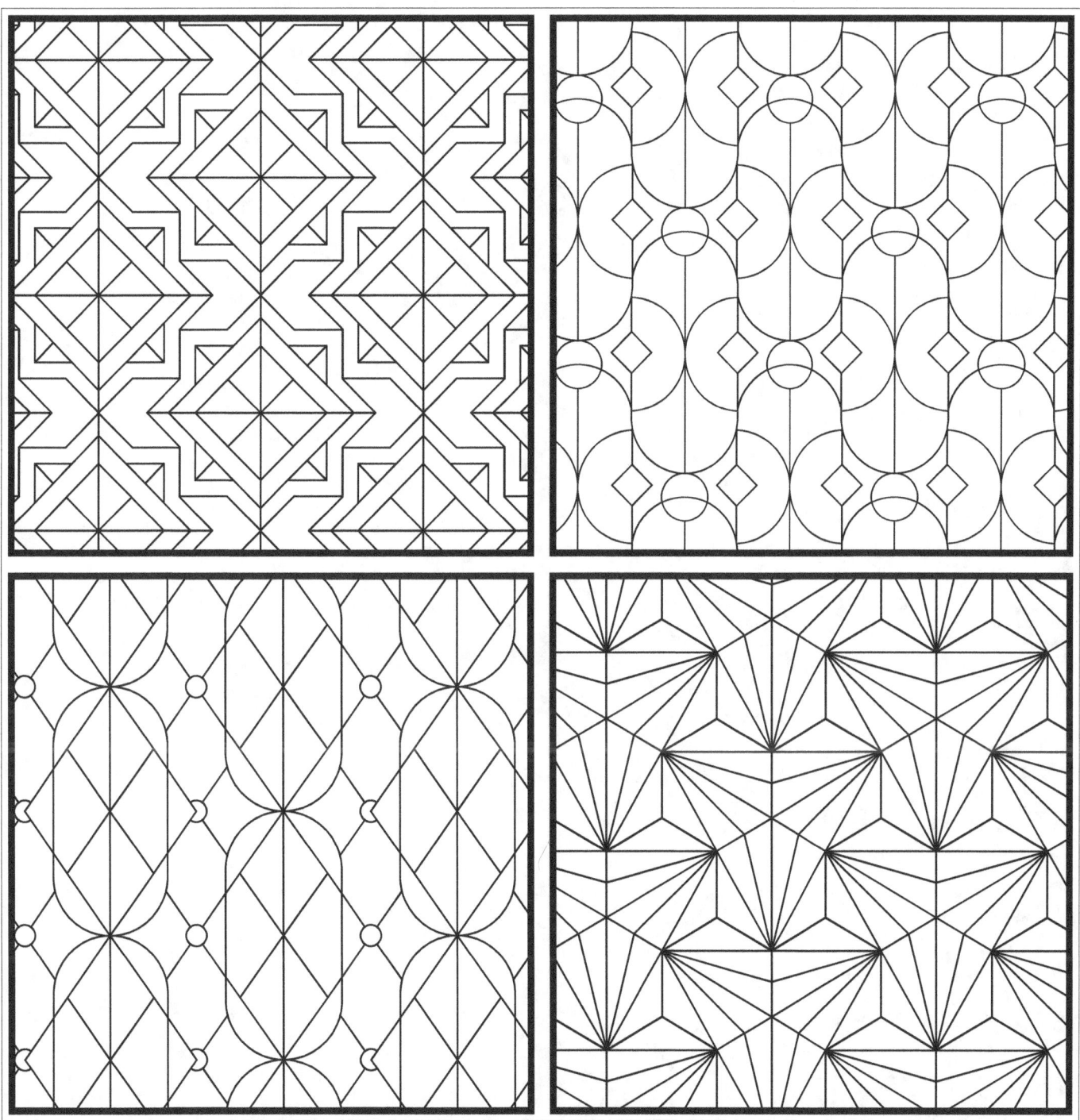

Imagine yourself in nature, finding a quiet spot near a gentle stream. Take off your shoes and dip your feet into the cool, refreshing water. Close your eyes and listen to the soothing sound of the flowing stream. Feel the water washing away your worries and stress. Allow yourself to be fully present in this peaceful moment. When you emerge from the water, feel a sense of calm and renewal. Carry the peacefulness of this experience with you, reminding yourself of the rejuvenating power of nature's embrace.

**19**

# Geometric Patterns

Echoing the diverse traditions and visual languages of various societies, patterns from different cultures tell stories of heritage and identity.

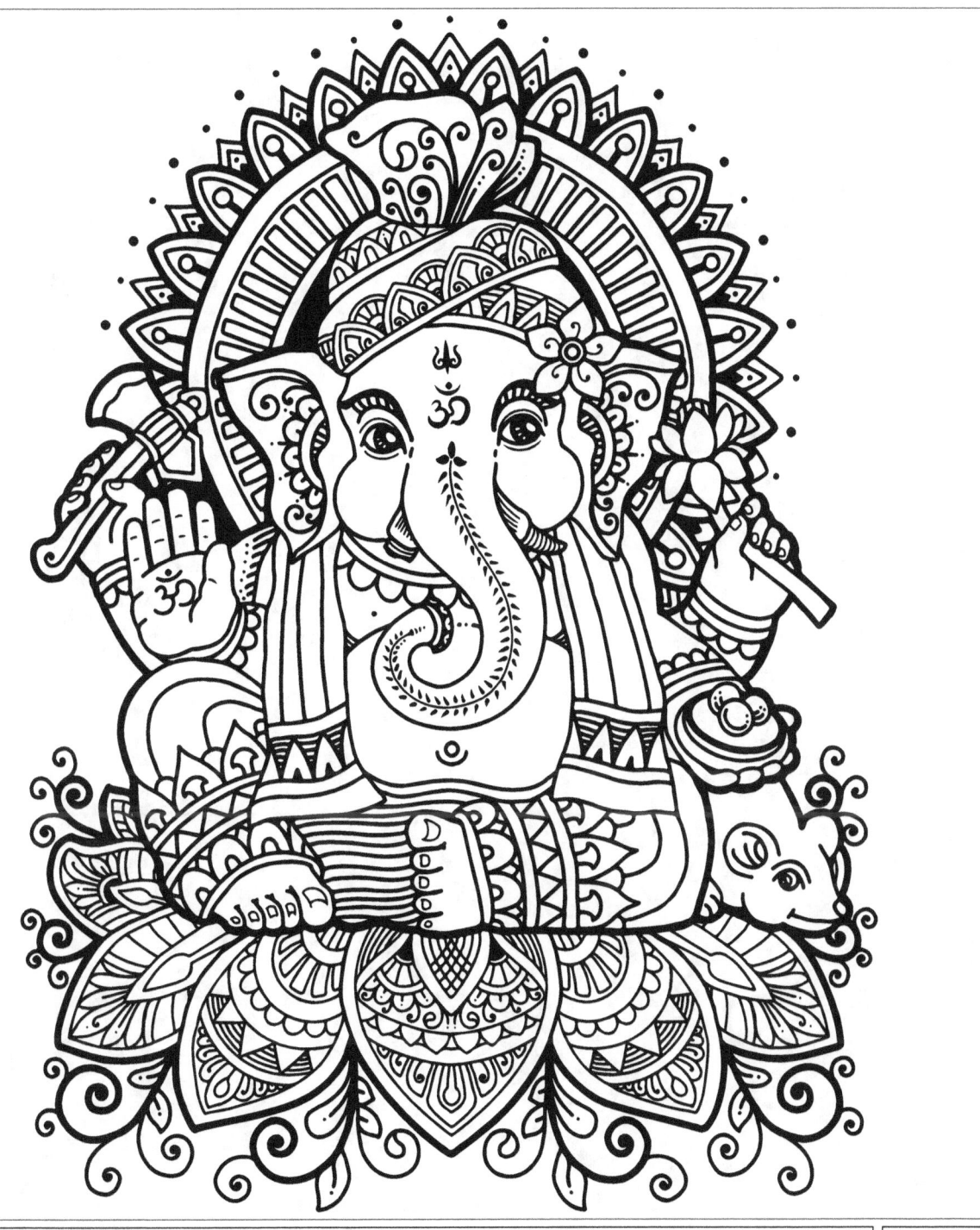

Imagine floating in a hot air balloon, high above a peaceful landscape. Look down and see the serene scenery below, with green fields, winding rivers, majestic mountains, and a shimmering lake reflecting the golden hues of the sunset. Feel the stillness in the air as you glide through the sky, with only the occasional call of a distant bird breaking the silence. Take a deep breath and appreciate the sense of calm in the moment, as the warm rays of the sun caress your skin. As the balloon descends, embrace the soothing ambiance you've experienced.

20

# Mythological Creatures

Inspired by ancient legends and folklore, coloring pages bring mythical creatures to life, igniting imagination and fascination with fantastical beings.

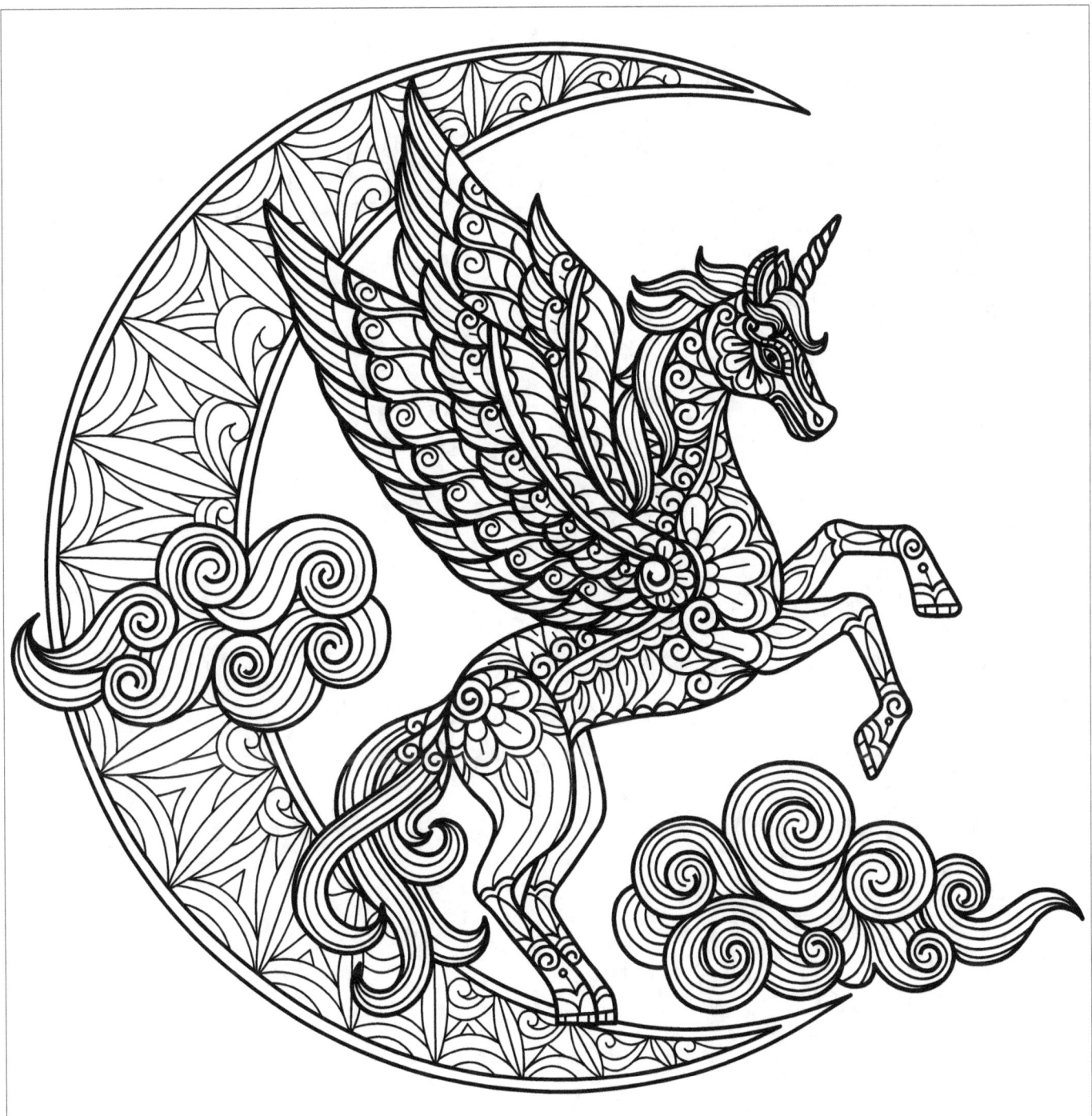

Close your eyes and listen to the birds singing their lively melodies. Let their joyful tunes transport you to a place of peace. Feel the gentle rhythm of their songs resonating within you, soothing your mind and uplifting your spirit. Breathe in the fresh air, filled with the sweet notes of nature's choir. Notice the different tones and patterns of their songs, as if they're engaged in a delightful conversation with one another. Allow their harmonies to create a serene backdrop for your thoughts and bring a sense of calm to your being.

21

# Underwater Scenes

Delving into the depths of the ocean, coloring pages capture the beauty and diversity of marine life, allowing individuals to explore the wonders of underwater ecosystems and their inhabitants.

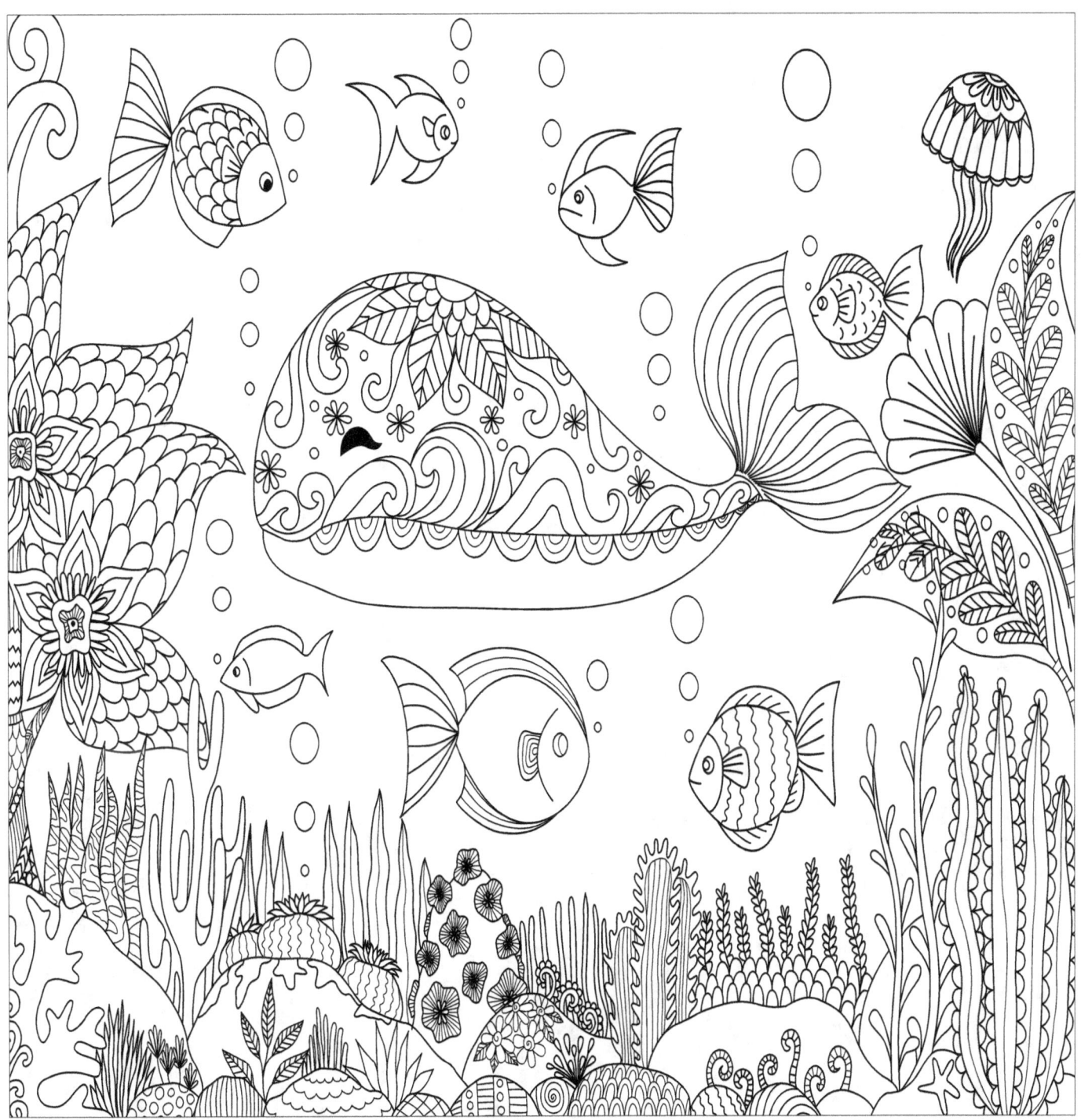

Imagine yourself by the ocean at sunset, practicing yoga. The sky is painted with warm colors as the sun sets. The sound of waves crashing creates a soothing rhythm. With each breath, the air from the ocean refreshes you. Moving through yoga poses, you feel connected to nature's energy. The peaceful setting helps release tension and worries. Sitting in quiet meditation, the fading light and gentle waves bring a sense of calm. As you stand up, carry the serenity of sunset yoga with you, embracing each day with a calm and centered spirit.

22

# Persian Rugs Design

Drawing from Persian culture, coloring pages showcase the intricate patterns and rich colors of Persian rugs, preserving the artistry and cultural heritage of this ancient tradition.

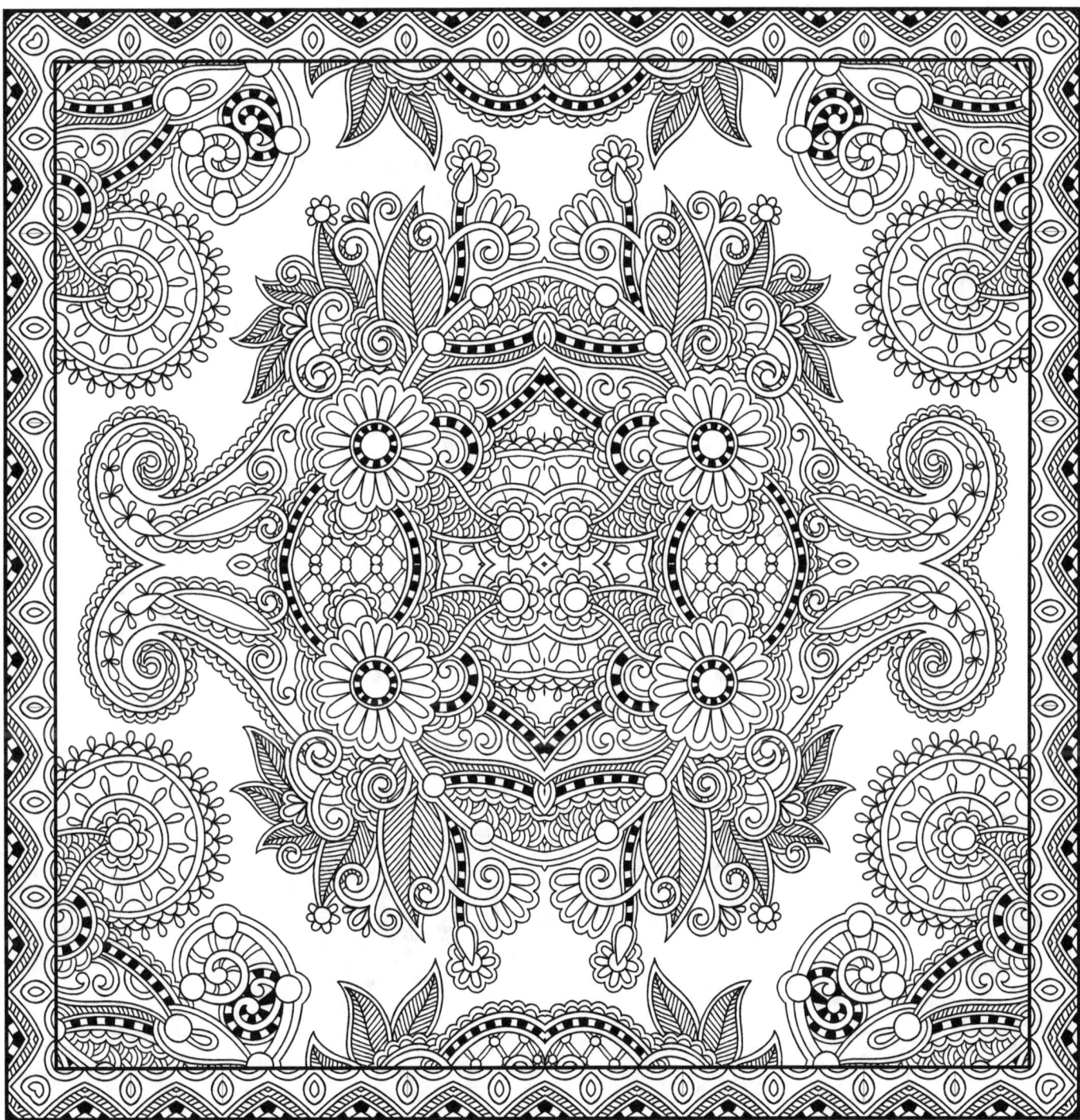

As the sun sets, find yourself by a calm lake. Watch as the sky's colors reflect on the water, creating a breathtaking sight. Take a deep breath and feel a sense of serenity wash over you. Listen to the gentle lapping of the water against the shore, creating a soothing rhythm. Let the beauty of the moment fill your heart and uplift your spirit. Embrace the peaceful ambiance as you witness the sunset's reflections on the lake, immersing yourself in the beauty of nature's artwork.

23

# Retro Design

Evoking nostalgia for past eras, coloring pages featuring retro designs transport individuals to a bygone time, celebrating vintage aesthetics and capturing the charm of yesteryears.

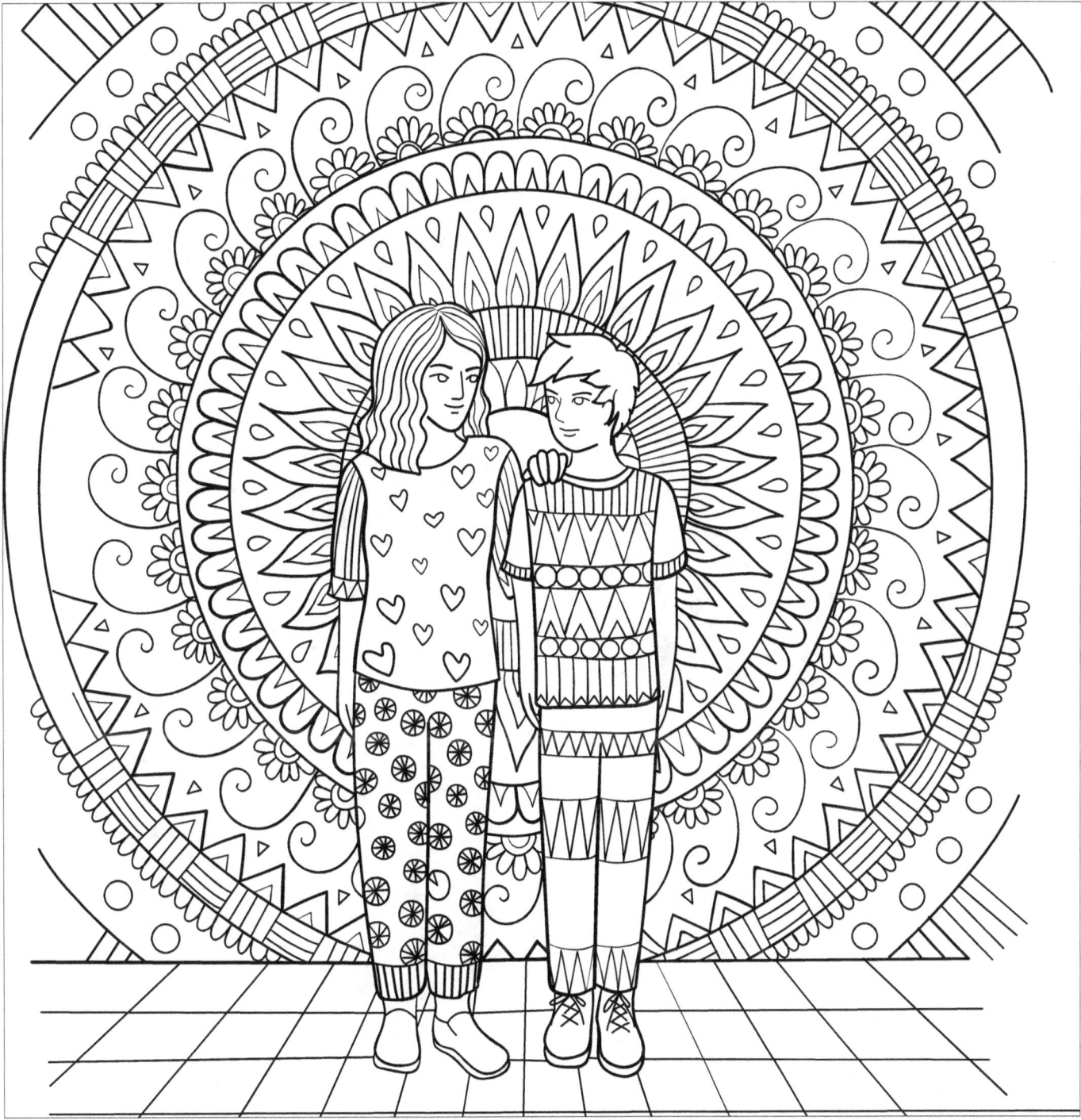

Sit in a peaceful terrace garden at dawn. Feel the gentle morning air as you take a deep breath. Notice the glistening dew on the plants and flowers, reflecting the soft light of the rising sun. Close your eyes and focus on your breath, allowing the fresh energy of the morning to invigorate your body. Embrace the stillness of the garden, hearing the distant chirping of birds adding a melodic touch to the serene ambiance. Take a moment to appreciate the vibrant colors, delicate scents, and the gentle touch of nature surrounding you.

24

# Psychedelic Art

Embracing vivid colors and abstract patterns, coloring pages inspired by psychedelic art create a mesmerizing and mind-altering experience, inviting individuals to explore the boundaries of imagination and creativity.

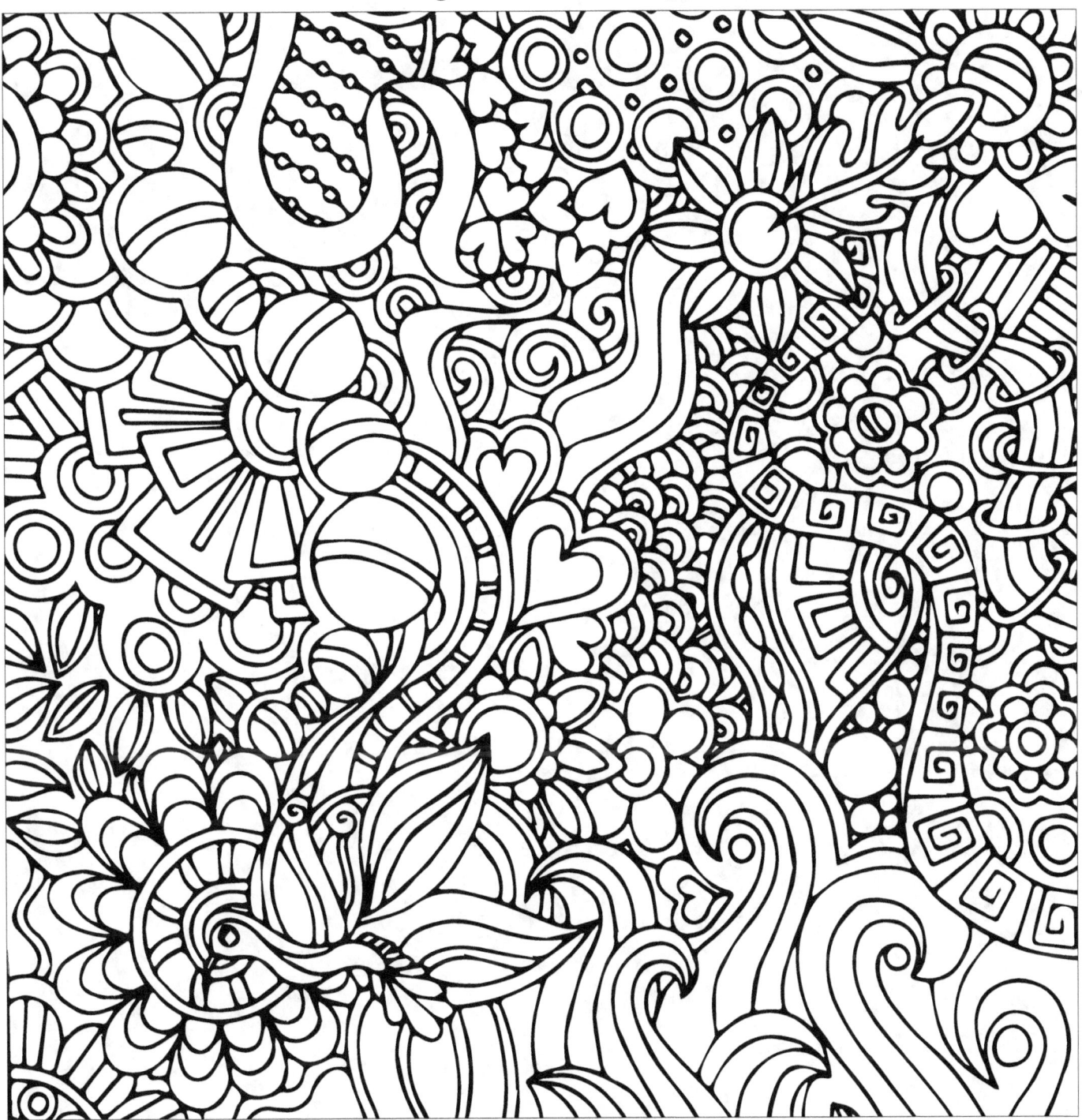

Immerse yourself in an enchanting rainforest soundscape. Close your eyes and imagine the gentle patter of raindrops and the melodic songs of tropical birds. Breathe in the earthy scent of damp soil and feel the cool mist on your skin. Feel a sense of peace as you connect with the natural world around you, surrounded by lush green foliage and vibrant flowers. Let the rhythmic sounds of trickling water and rustling leaves lull you into a state of deep relaxation. Allow the rainforest's serenity to embrace you, as nature offers a soothing embrace.

**25**

# Whimsical Landscapes

Unleashing a sense of wonder and enchantment, coloring pages with whimsical landscapes transport individuals to magical worlds filled with imaginative elements, sparking joy and creativity.

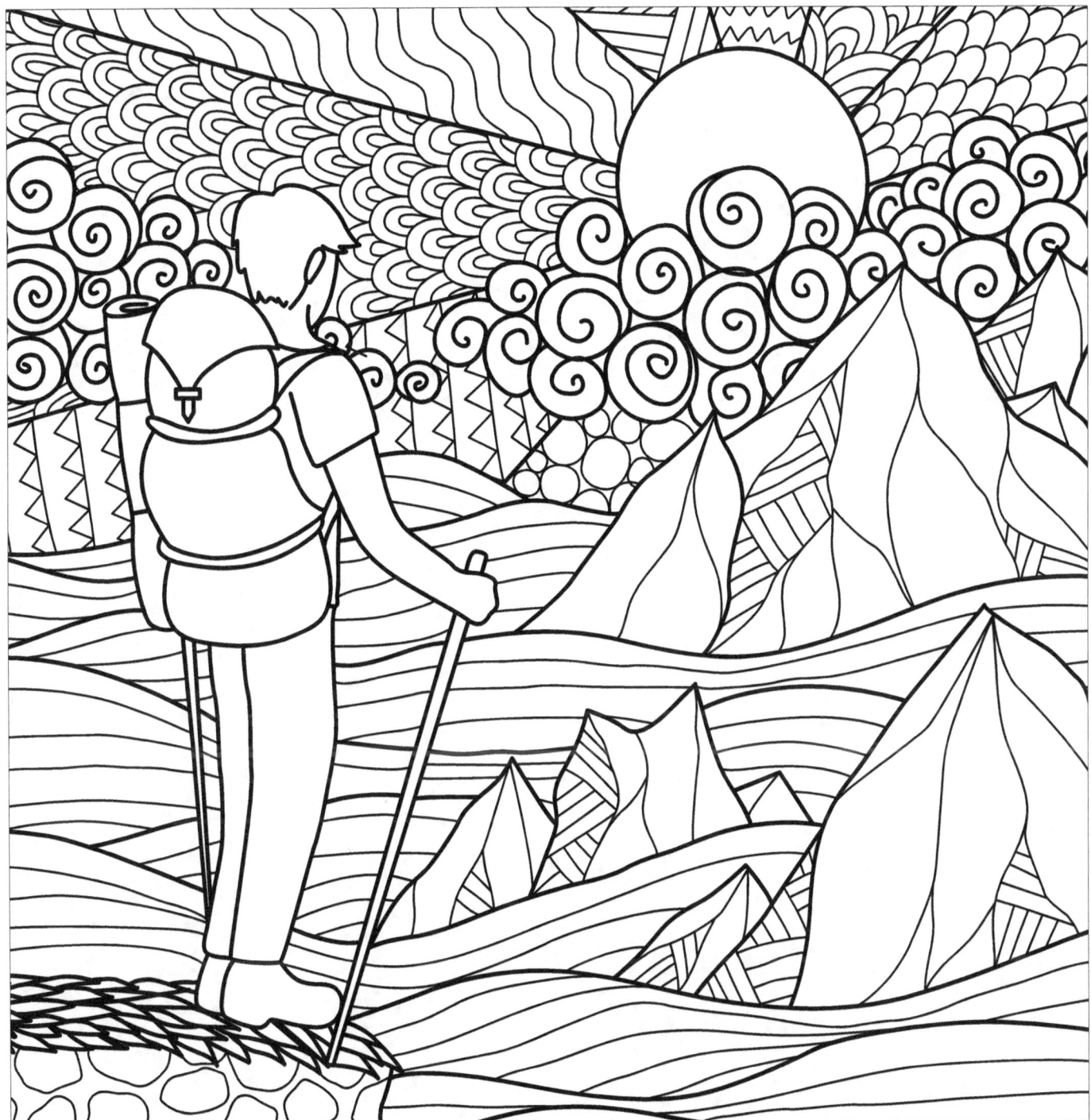

Look up at the starry night sky and let your worries fade away. Take a deep breath and imagine yourself floating among the twinkling stars. Feel the peace and wonder of the universe as you listen to the soothing sounds of nature around you. Hear the gentle rustle of leaves, the distant chirping of nocturnal creatures, the rhythmic clapping of waves in the distance, and the soft crackling of a campfire nearby. Let the calming energy envelop you and find solace in the infinite beauty of the night sky.

26

# Portraits

Capturing the essence of individuals, coloring pages featuring portraits provide a canvas to express emotions and explore the depth of human expression, allowing colorists to create personal connections and artistic interpretations.

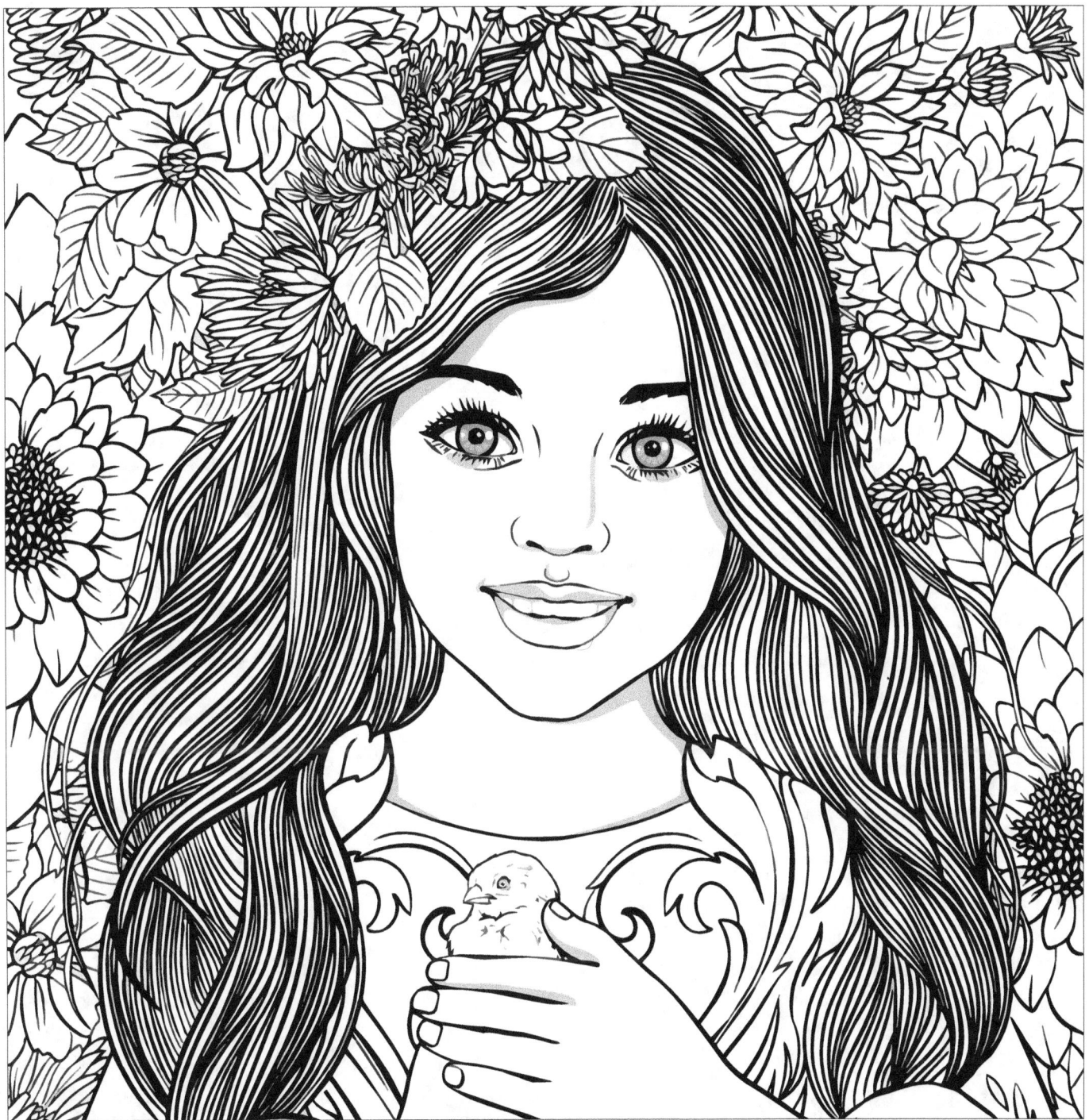

Imagine yourself gently floating on a serene lotus pond, surrounded by vibrant lily pads and delicate blossoms. Feel the cool water caressing your skin as you lay back and let go of all tension. Listen to the gentle ripples and the subtle symphony of chirping frogs, buzzing dragonflies, the distant rustle of leaves, and the soothing melody of wind chimes nearby. Look up at the night sky and marvel at the blanket of twinkling stars, illuminating the darkness with their celestial beauty. Allow yourself to be carried away by the peacefulness of this enchanting oasis.

27

# Optical Illusions

Intriguing visual phenomena that challenge perception, as a person encountered a mind-bending illusion, now explored through coloring to stimulate creativity and explore visual trickery.

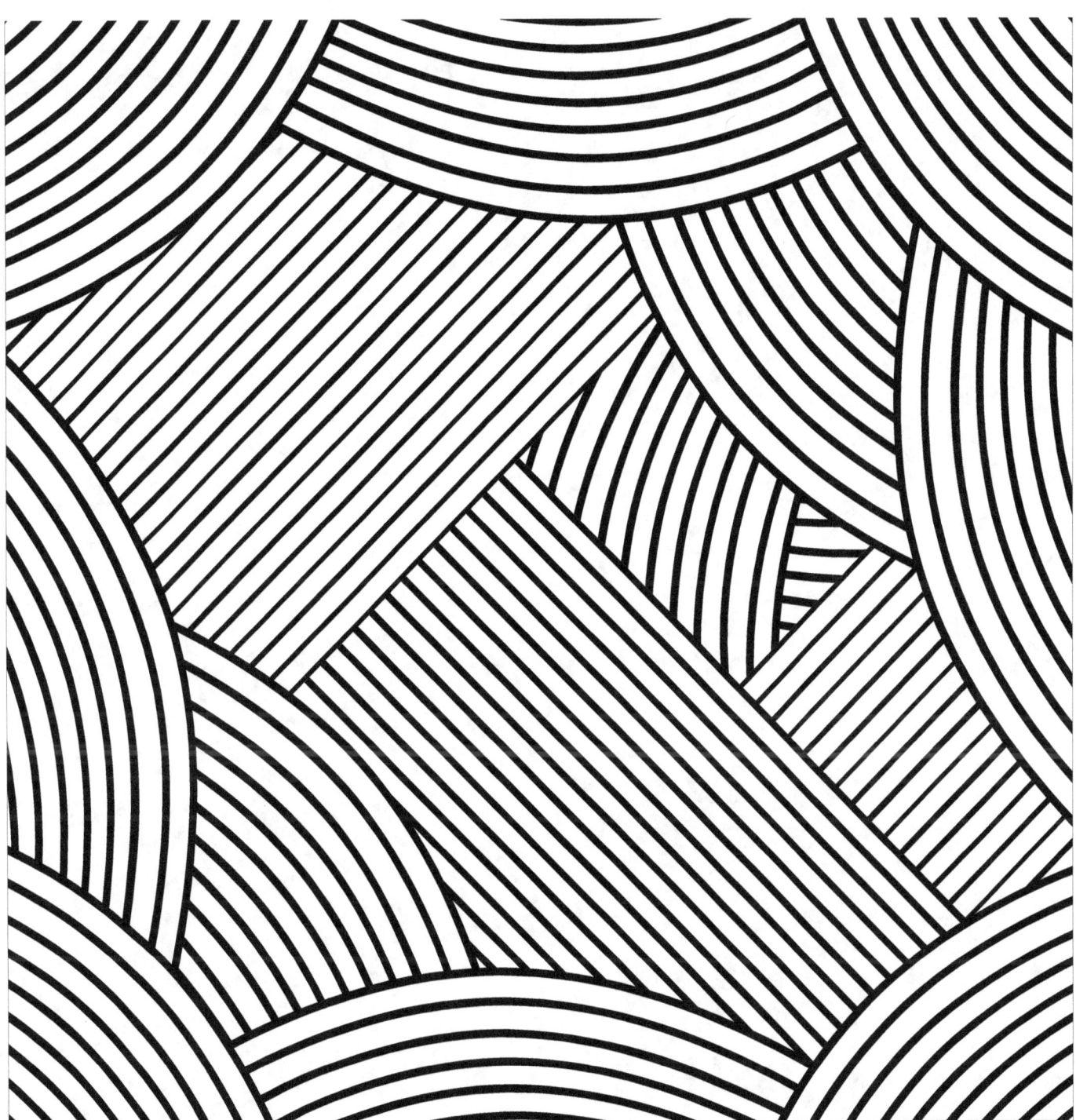

Imagine yourself lying in a comfortable hammock, gently swaying in the rhythm of nature. Feel the soft fabric supporting your body as you surrender to its gentle movement. With each swing, let go of any worries or stress, allowing yourself to be fully present in the moment. Listen to the melodic songs of birds and the rustling of leaves, creating a symphony of natural sounds. Embrace the feeling of weightlessness and relaxation as you drift into a state of pure calm, enveloped by the serene atmosphere of this suspended retreat.

**28**

# Tribal Patterns

Ancient designs reflecting cultural identity, as an archaeologist uncovered beautifully carved tribal symbols, now celebrated through coloring to preserve indigenous artistry and appreciate tribal heritage.

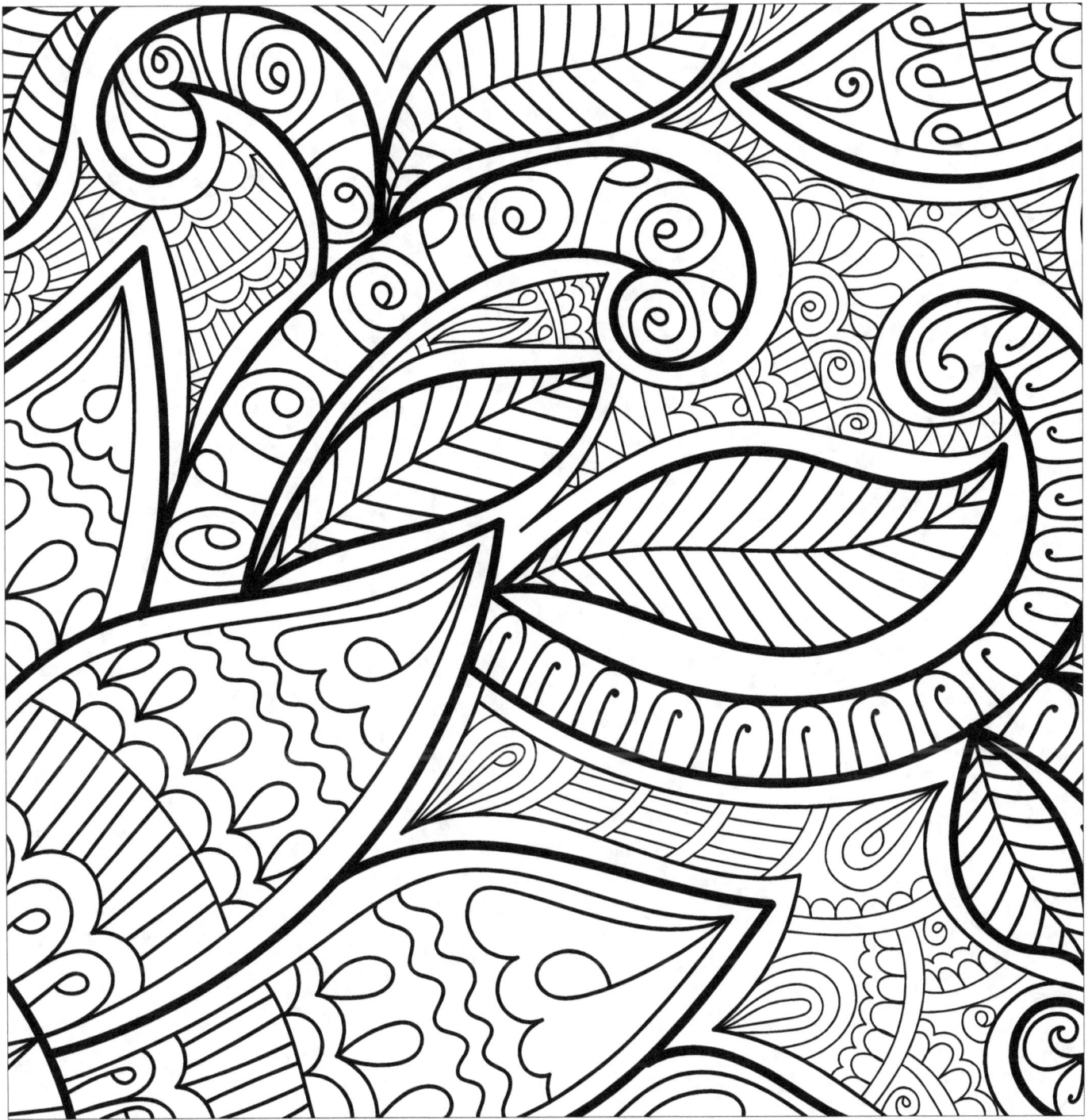

Picture yourself sitting by a crackling campfire, the warm glow casting a soft light on your surroundings. Feel the gentle heat against your skin as you settle into a comfortable position. Close your eyes and take a deep breath, allowing the aroma of burning wood to fill your senses. Listen to the soothing crackling and popping sounds as the fire dances before you. As you let go of tension and worries, feel the weight of the day melting away. Allow the flickering flames to mesmerize you, guiding you into a deep state of relaxation.

29

# Sacred Geometry Patterns

Symbolic patterns embodying cosmic order, as temple floor designs revealed the harmony of sacred geometry, now embraced through coloring to connect with spirituality and explore geometric symbolism.

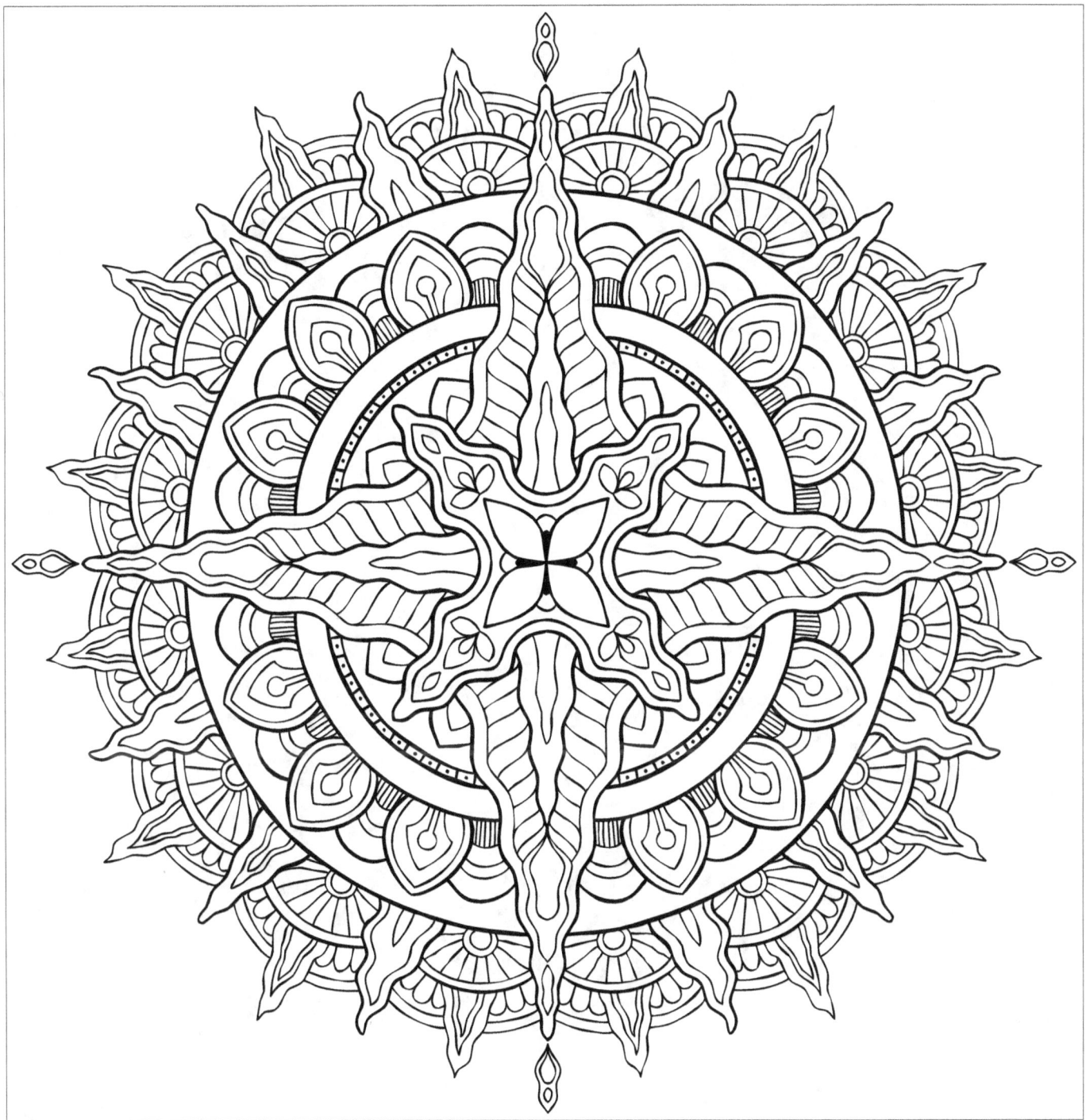

Picture yourself surrounded by towering bamboo trees in a peaceful forest. The bamboo stalks stand tall and steady, creating a sense of calm. The air is still and quiet, allowing you to fully immerse yourself in the peacefulness of the surroundings. As you stroll through the forest, you can feel the gentle touch of the soft ground beneath your feet, grounding you in the present moment. Take slow, deep breaths, inhaling the fresh forest air, and exhale any tension or worries. Find comfort in the serene atmosphere of the bamboo forest, letting go of any distractions.

**30**

# Space Exploration

Expanding human knowledge beyond Earth's boundaries, as astronauts beheld the breathtaking view of our planet from space, now captured through coloring to inspire cosmic wonder and appreciation for the vast universe.

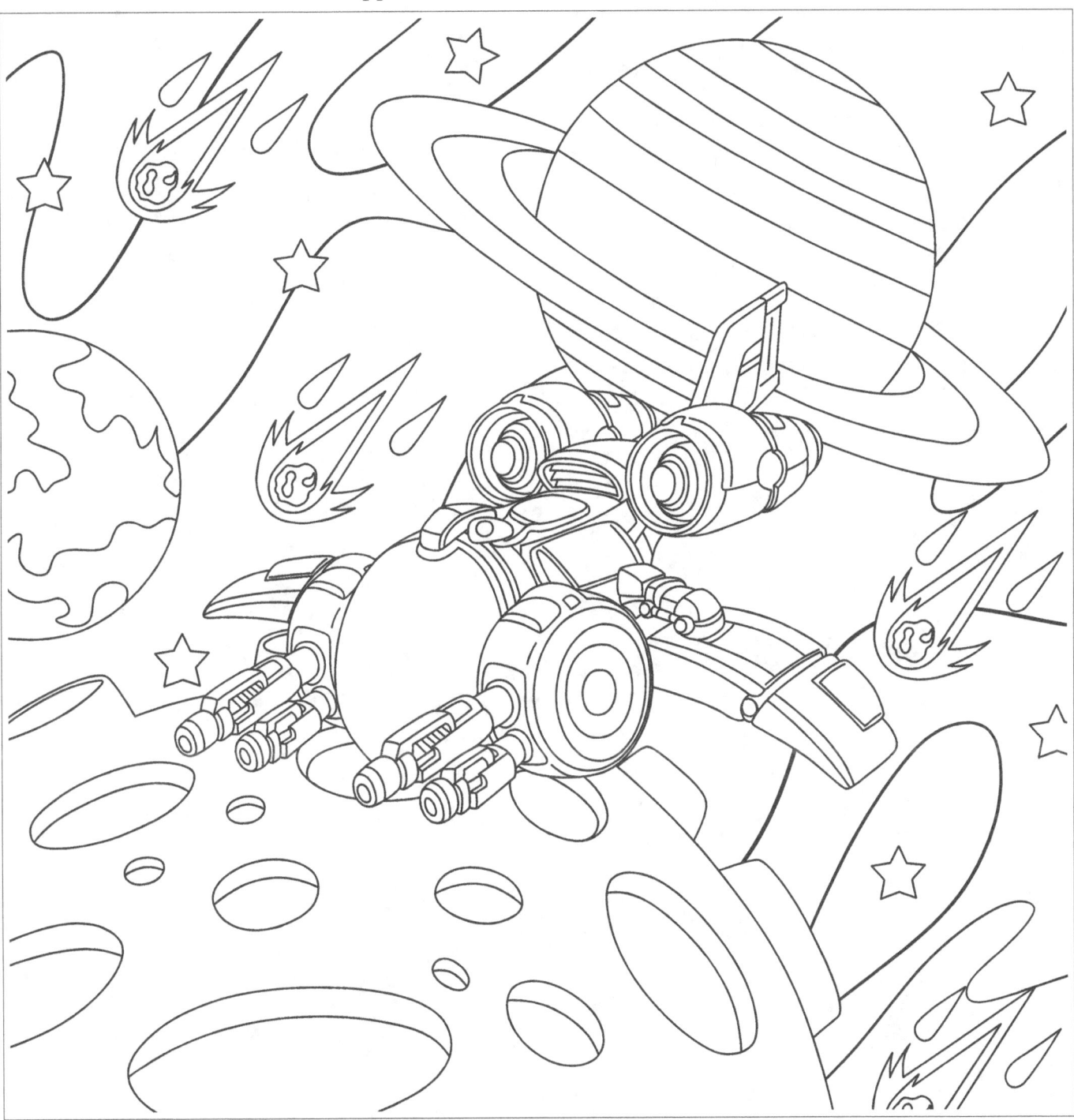

·Close your eyes and imagine floating through space. Visualize yourself amidst a breathtaking scene of swirling colors and cosmic wonders. Feel the weightlessness as you navigate the vast expanse, surrounded by shimmering stars and celestial wonders. Allow yourself to become one with the cosmic energy and infinite possibilities that surround you. Breathe in the limitless energy of the cosmos. Embrace the profound sense of serenity and connection to the boundless universe. Open your eyes, carrying this inner peace with you, knowing that you are part of something greater.

31

# Zodiac Sign

Astrological symbols representing individual traits, as someone discovered their unique zodiac constellation, now expressed through coloring as a personal connection to astrological influences.

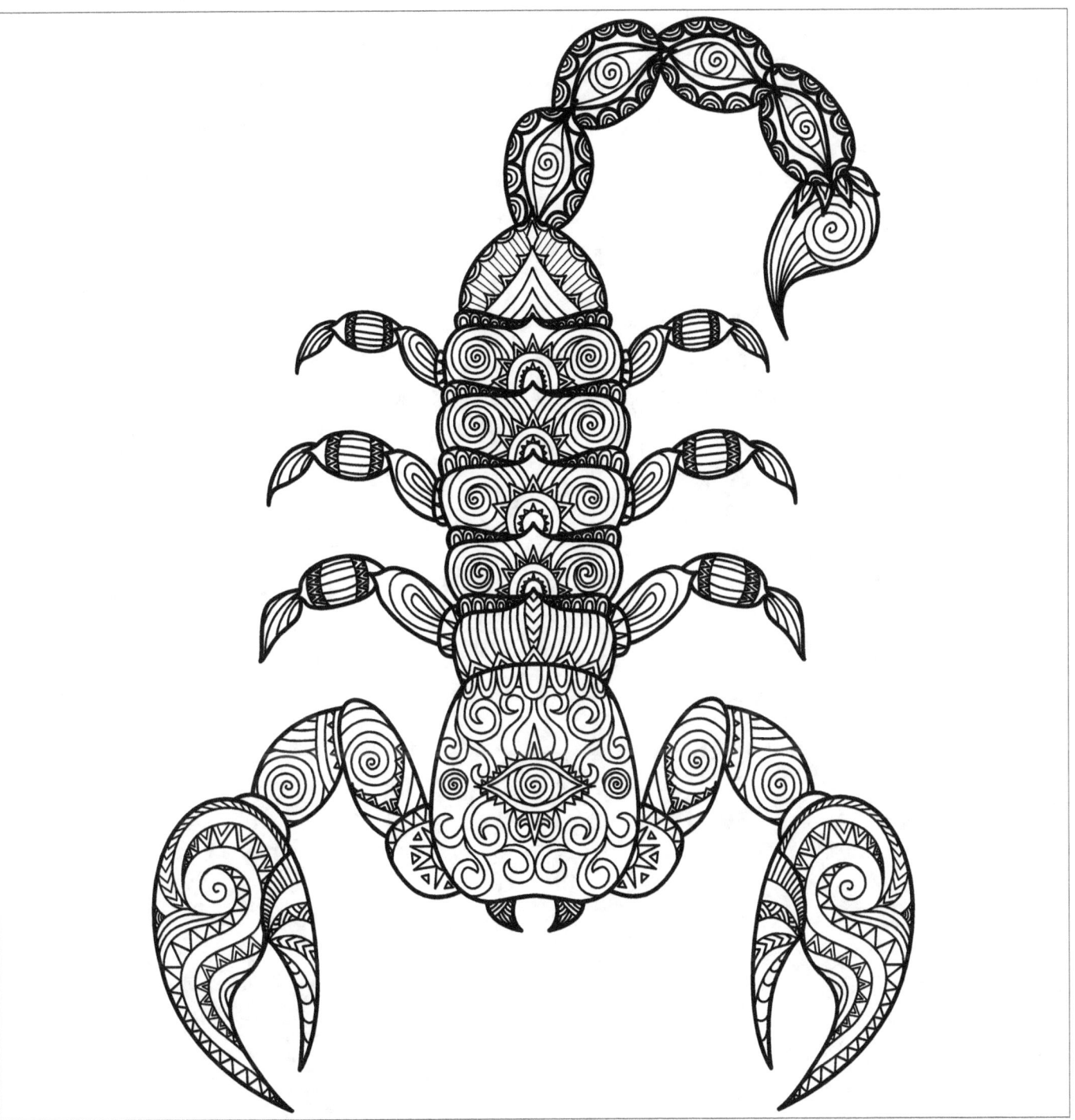

Imagine standing in a field of golden sunflowers, their vibrant petals reaching towards the sky. Stand amidst a golden field of sunflowers, their faces basking in the warm sunlight. The warm sun bathes the landscape in a soft glow, creating a peaceful ambiance. As you breathe in, the sweet scent of the sunflowers fills the air, rejuvenating your senses. Take a moment to feel the stillness around you, as the sunflowers stand tall and motionless. Allow the beauty of this serene scene to calm your mind and bring a sense of peace to your being.

32

# Celtic Knot Work

Intricate interwoven patterns from Celtic culture, as historians uncovered beautifully adorned manuscripts, now treasured through coloring to preserve Celtic artistry and honor cultural heritage.

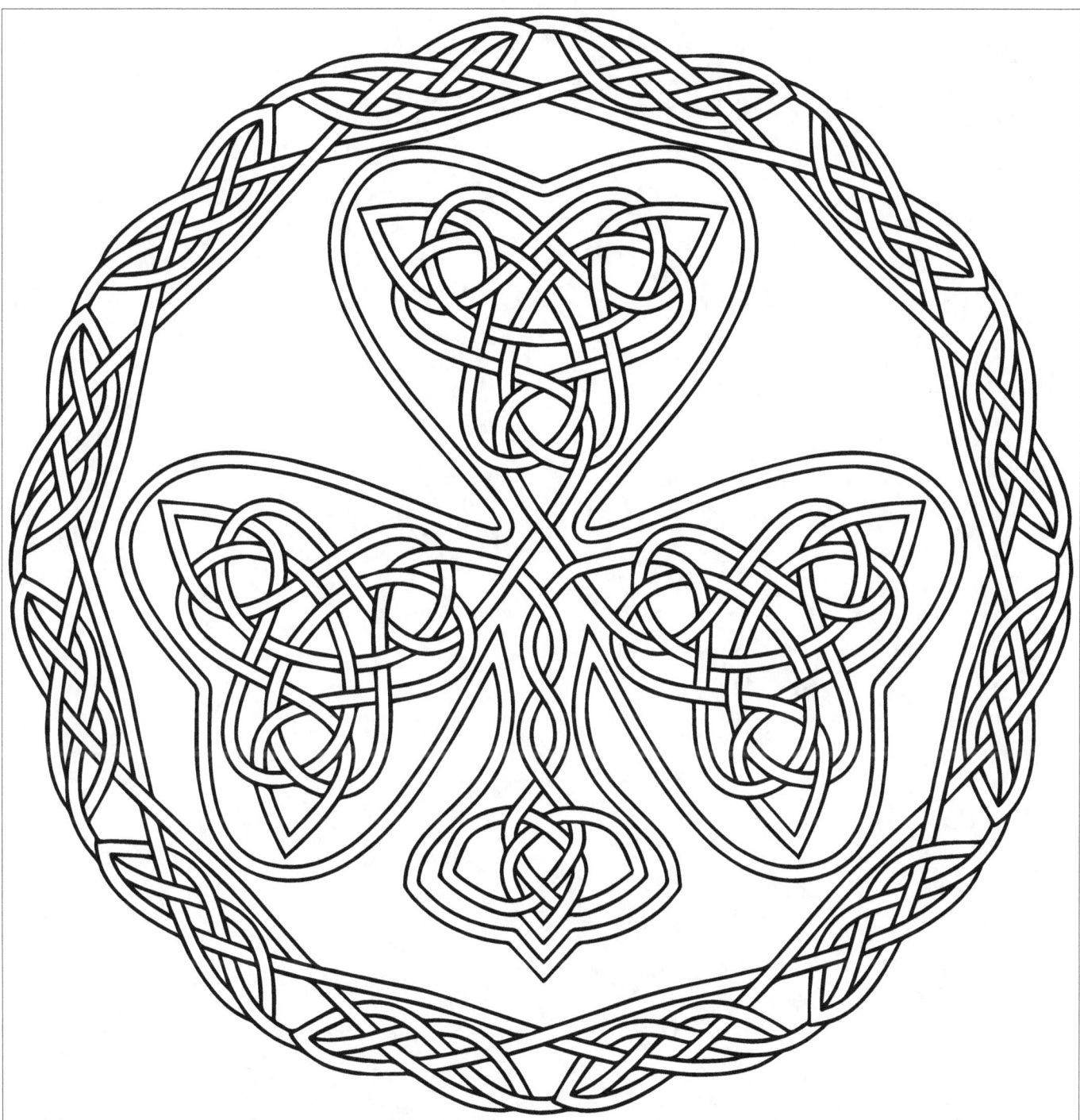

Let your senses come alive as you fully engage with the sights, sounds, and scents around you. Let go of the past and release worries about the future. Breathe deeply, feeling the air fill your lungs and exhaling any tension. Be fully present in this moment, embracing its simplicity and richness. Surrender to the here and now, where peace and contentment reside. Allow yourself to let go and immerse in the beauty and possibilities of the present, where every breath brings clarity and freedom.

33

# Tree of Life

Symbolizing interconnectedness and the cycle of existence, as a traveler stood beneath a majestic ancient tree, now celebrated through coloring as a representation of life's beauty and interdependence.

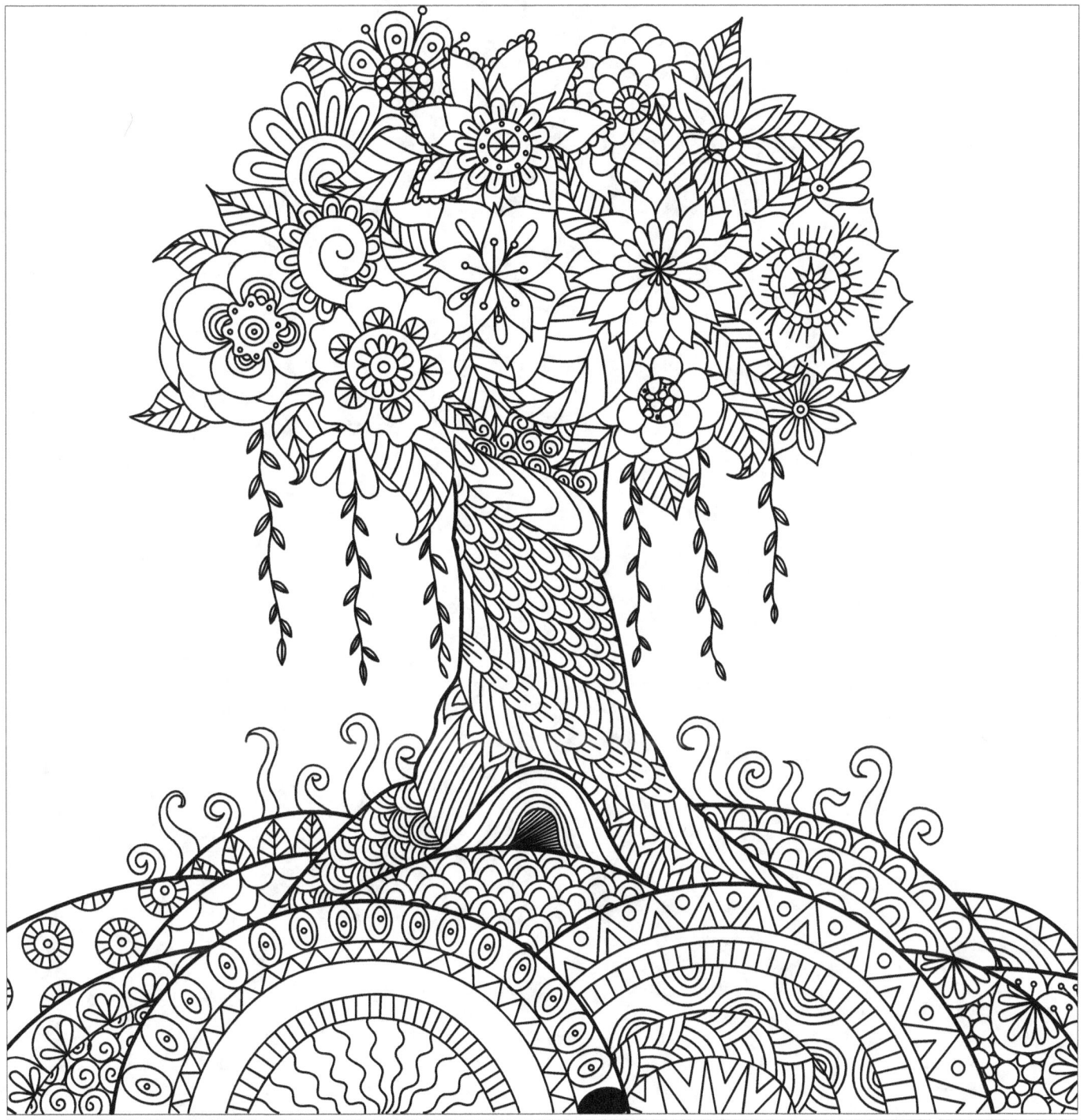

Imagine the ocean waves gently lapping against the shore. Listen to their soothing sound as they come and go. Feel the coolness of the water on your feet and the soft sand beneath you. Breathe in the salty air and let it relax your body and calm your mind. Take a moment to absorb the peacefulness of the ocean, letting go of any worries or stress. Allow yourself to be fully present in this serene moment, finding peace in the gentle rhythm of the waves.

**34**

# Pagodas

Serene Asian architectural structures, as wanderers marveled at the design of pagodas amidst peaceful gardens, now admired and colored to capture the tranquility and cultural richness they embody.

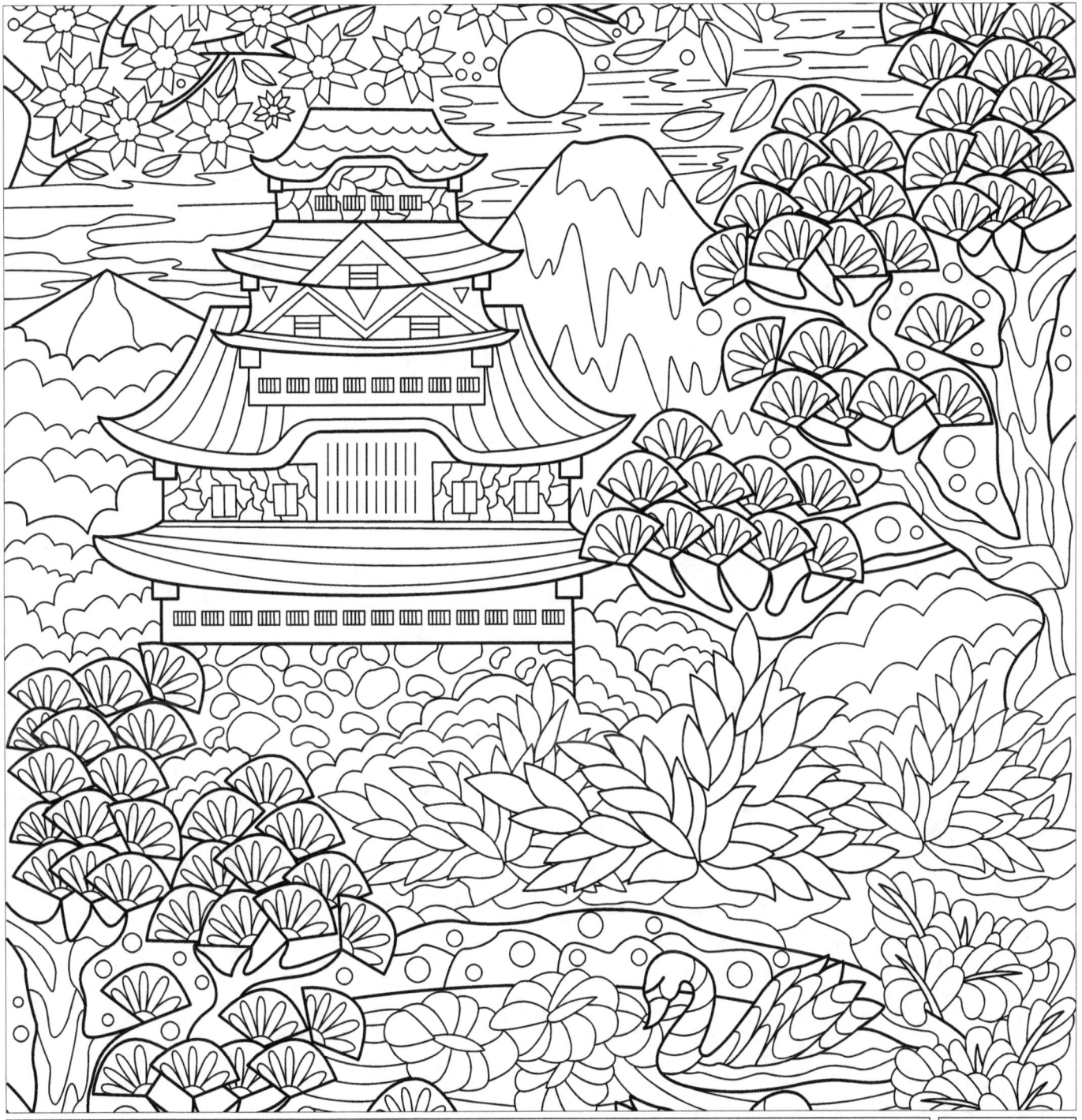

Sit by a peaceful Zen pond. Close your eyes and feel the warm sun on your skin. Hear the calming sounds of flowing water and birds singing. Take deep breaths, letting go of stress and worries. Be fully present in this moment, enjoying the quiet and calm. Offer a heartfelt prayer to God, sharing your intentions and gratitude. Let go of all burdens, trusting in divine guidance. Feel a deep sense of inner peace washing over you, like gentle ripples on the pond.

**35**

# Dream Catcher

Native American tradition of protective charms, as storytellers shared legends of dream catchers, now cherished through coloring, embracing their symbolism and spiritual significance.

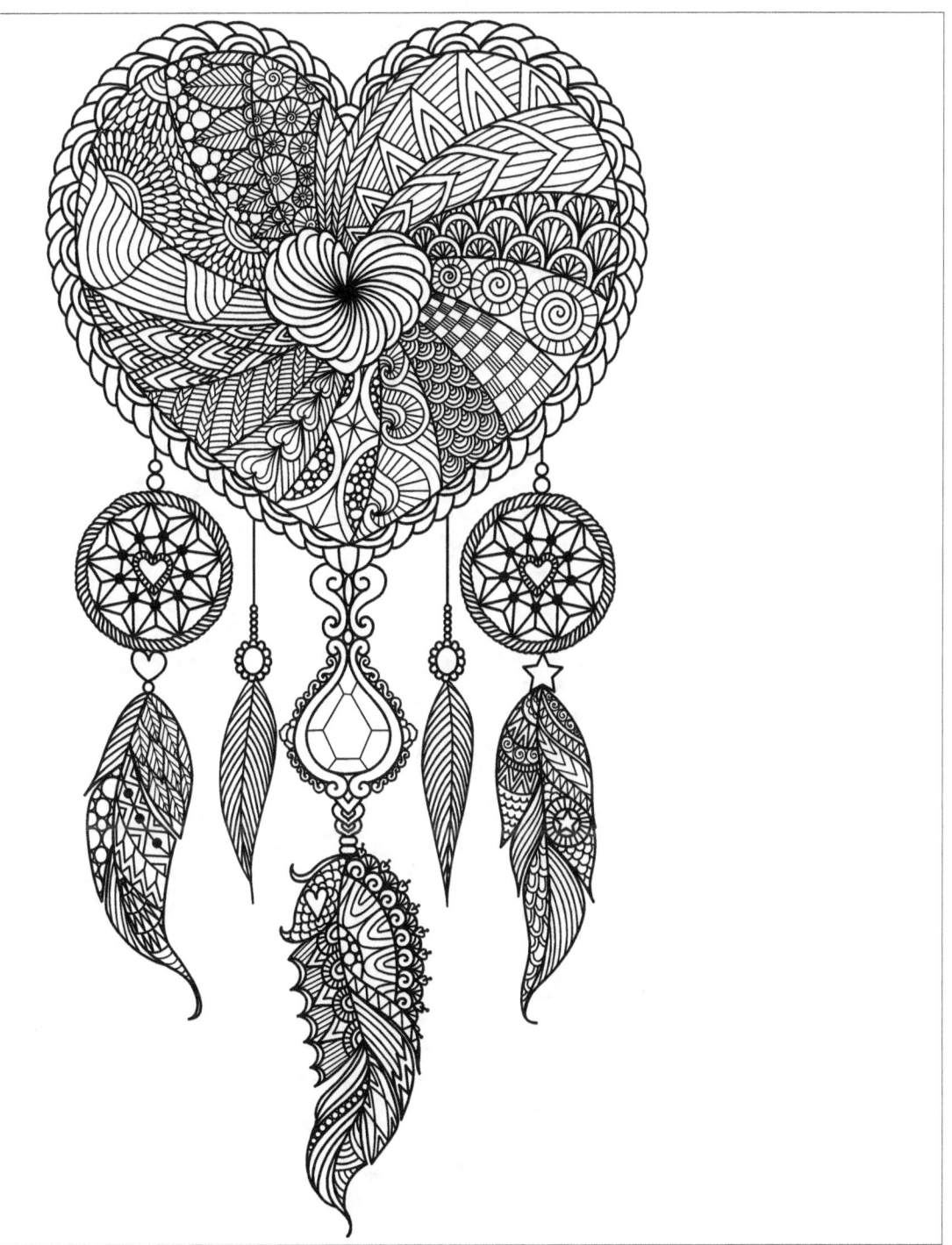

Imagine yourself on a peaceful balcony, with chimes gently moving in the wind. Close your eyes and listen to their calming sounds. Feel the gentle vibrations as the chimes touch each other, creating a sense of calmness. Let the wind carry their beautiful sounds to your ears. Allow the chimes to bring harmony and peace to your mind. Experience the serenity as the chimes sing, creating a soothing atmosphere. When you open your eyes, carry the peaceful feeling of the chimes with you, finding balance in your everyday life.

**36**

# Henna

Ancient art form adorning the body with intricate designs, as a bride celebrated her wedding with elaborately decorated henna patterns, now enjoyed through coloring to appreciate the beauty and cultural heritage of henna art.

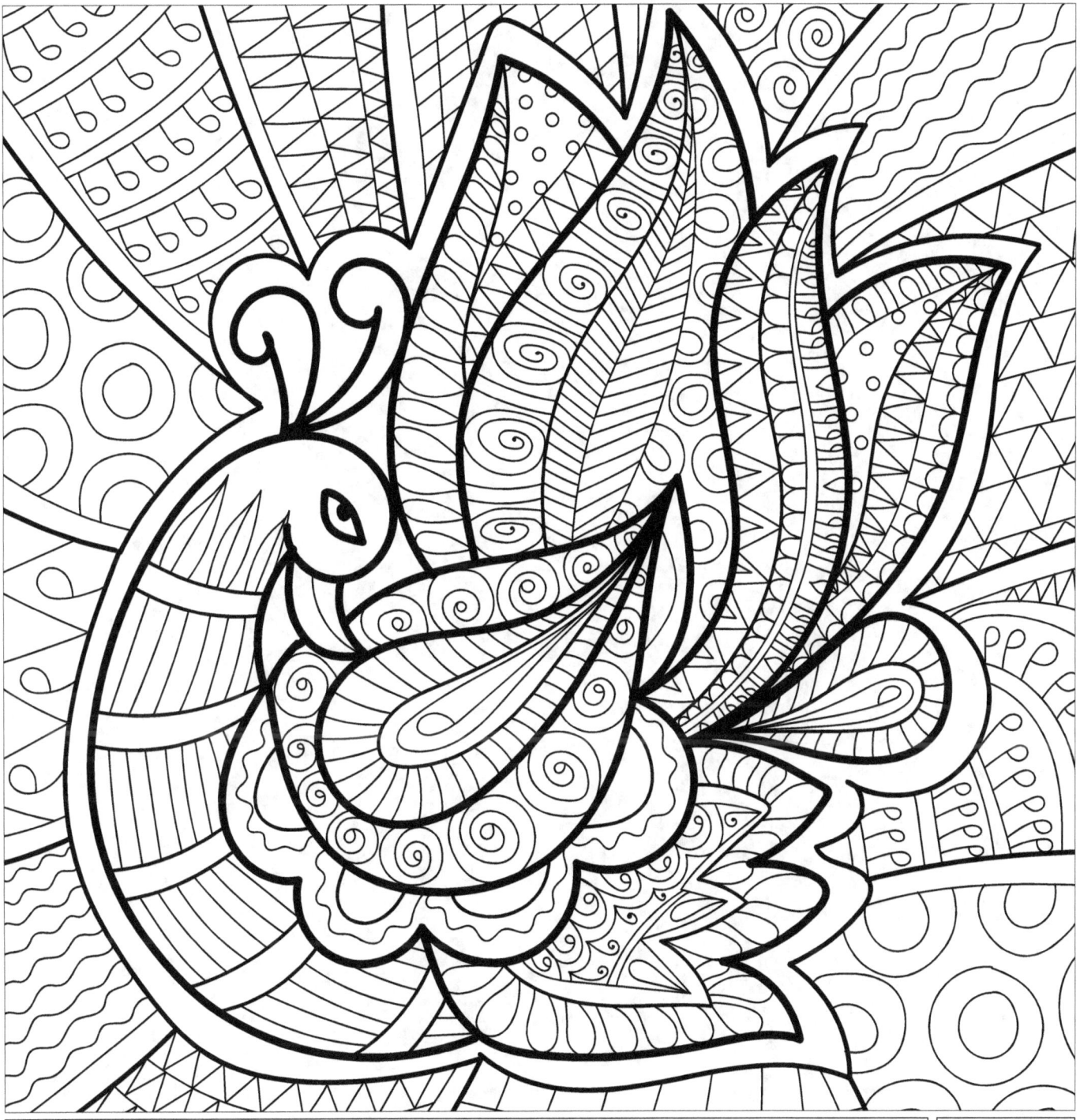

Imagine standing at the base of a majestic lighthouse, its towering presence commanding your attention. Begin climbing the spiral staircase, each step bringing you closer to the top. Arriving at the summit, take a moment to absorb the breathtaking panoramic view of the vast ocean and the endless horizon. Let the guiding light of the lighthouse fill you with a sense of clarity and direction. Allow its steady beam to illuminate your path, guiding you towards your aspirations and dreams. Embrace the knowledge that you have the power to navigate through life's challenges and reach new heights.

37

# Enchanted Forest Scenes

Inspired by folklore and nature, coloring pages depict magical forest settings, transporting individuals to a realm of wonder and imagination.

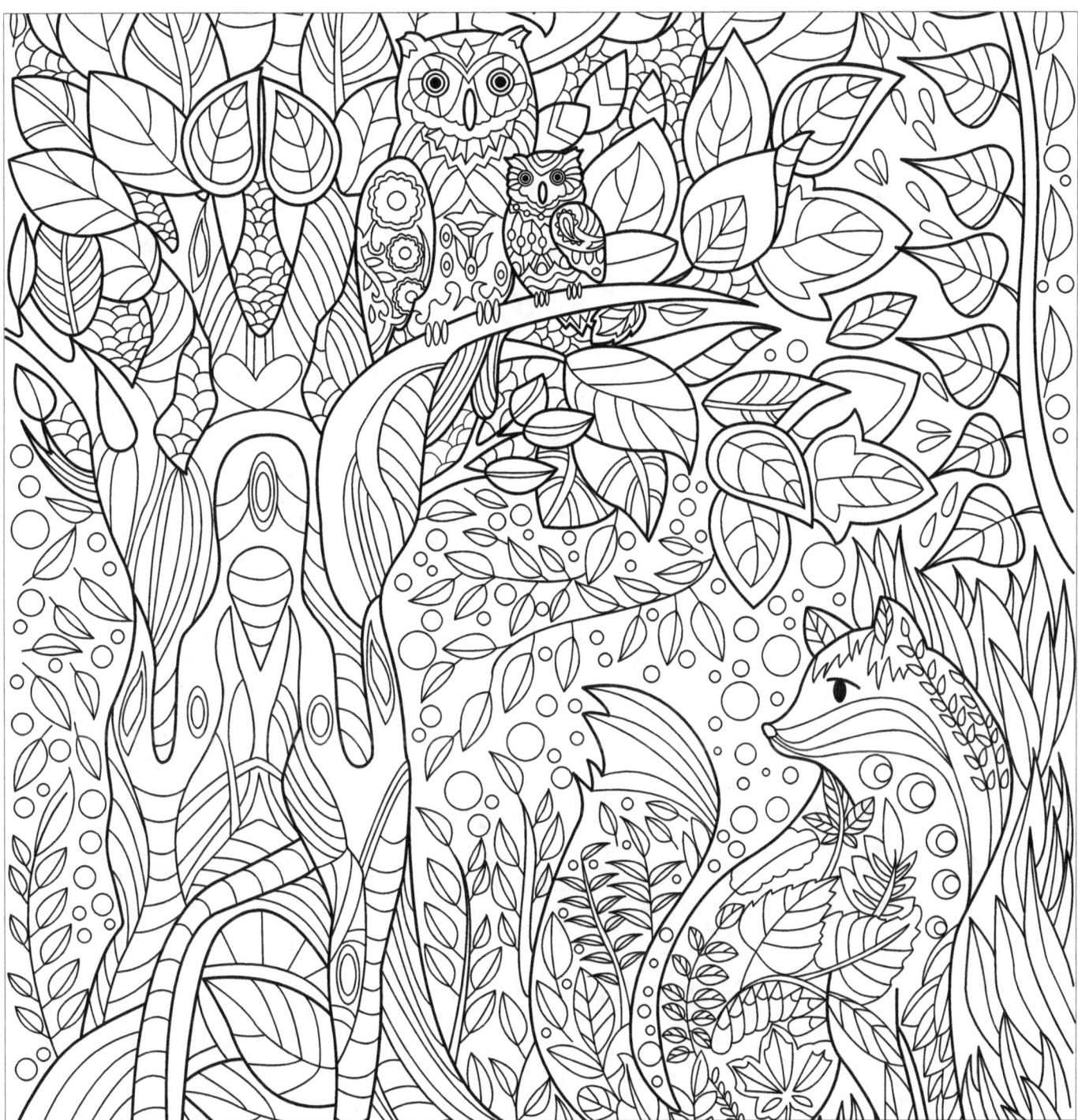

Imagine standing on a tall cliff by the ocean. The waves crash against the rocks with a strong and calming sound. Feel the mist from the waves on your face. Let the ocean's energy calm your mind and body. The sound of the waves washes away any worries or stress. Embrace the power of the ocean and let it bring you peace. Let go of tension and surrender to the natural rhythm of life. Find comfort in the beauty of the ocean and remember your own strength.

**38**

# Mysterious

Embracing an aura of intrigue, coloring pages with enigmatic symbols and hidden elements invite individuals to unravel secrets and create their own narratives.

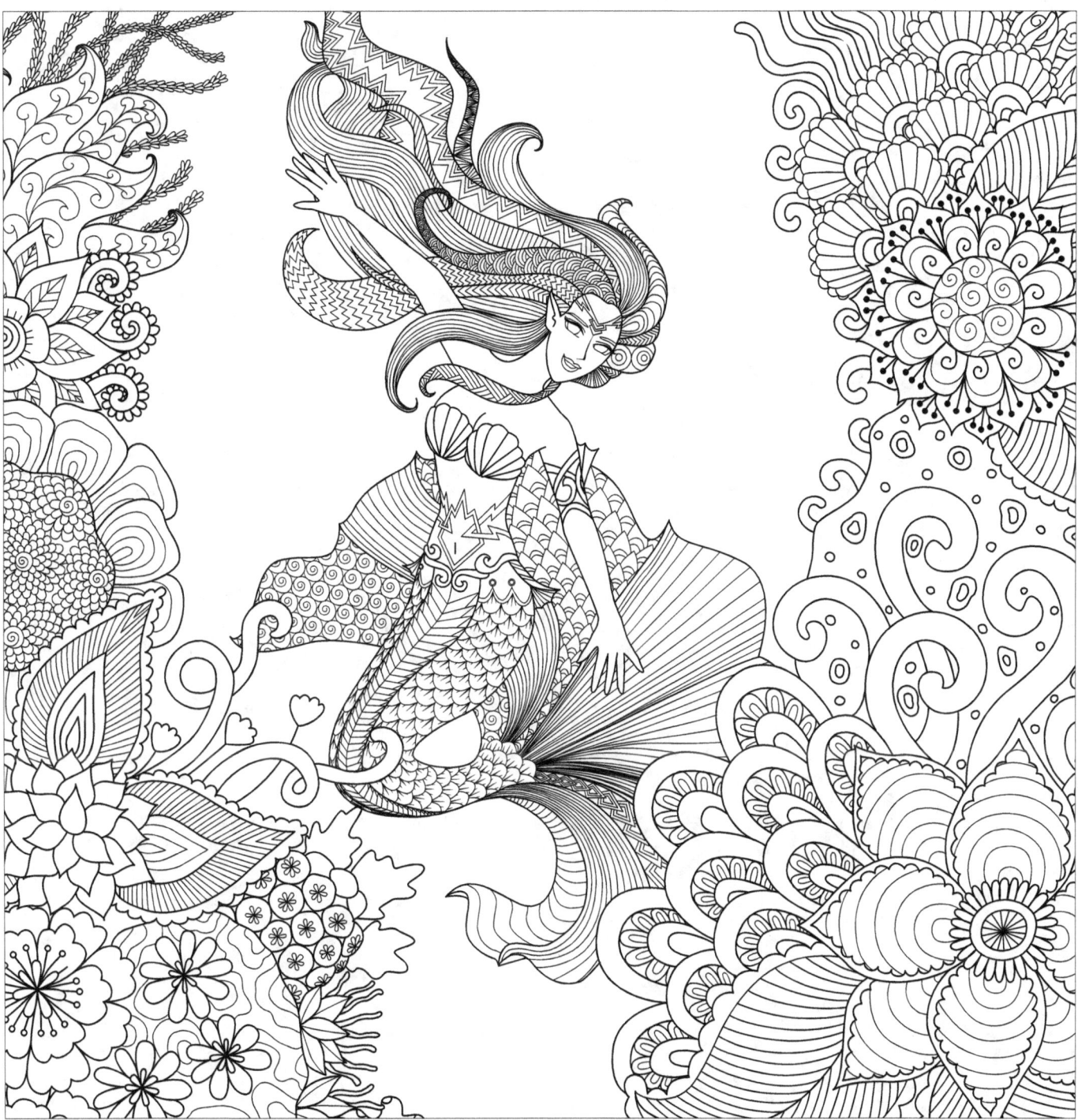

Imagine walking along a winding forest path, surrounded by the peacefulness of nature, as it leads you to a hidden gem—Buddha temple nestled amidst the trees. The soothing sound of a nearby stream whispers a calming melody, adding to the harmony of the surroundings. The scent of moss and earth fills the air, grounding you in the present moment. As you approach the temple, the soft chiming of wind chimes greets your ears, inviting you to enter this sacred space of peace and contemplation. Here, amidst the ancient trees and the timeless wisdom embodied by the Buddha statue.

39

# Surreal Landscapes

Unleashing the power of imagination, coloring pages feature dreamlike and otherworldly landscapes, blurring the boundaries between reality and fantasy.

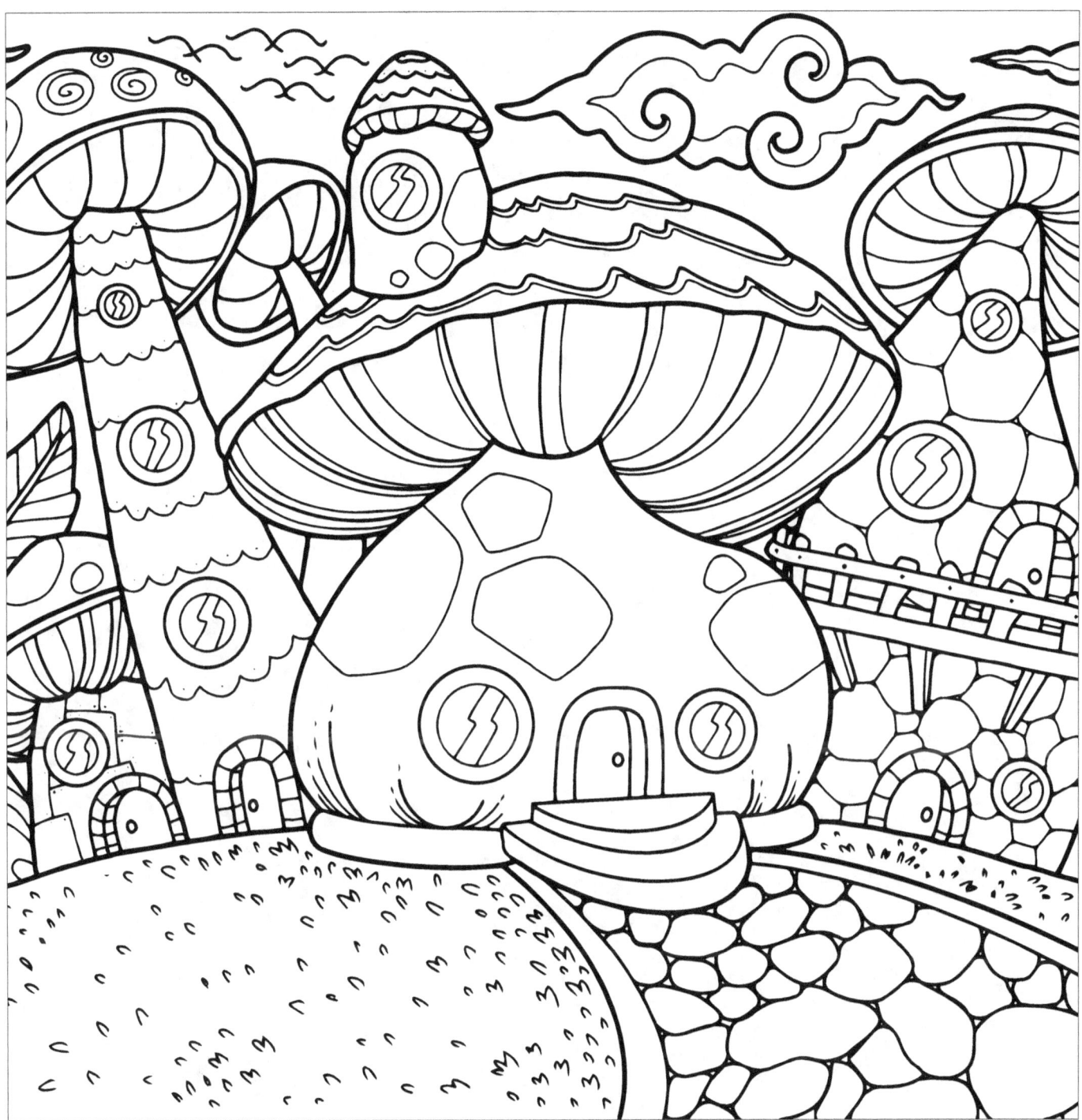

Picture yourself in a winter wonderland, where the air is crisp and the world is transformed by a gentle snowfall. Delicate snowflakes twirl and dance as they descend from the sky, creating a magical atmosphere. The landscape is adorned with a fresh layer of snow, covering everything in a white coat. The trees, with their branches draped in glistening snow, create a stunning sight. As you stand there, surrounded by the hushed stillness, you can't help but feel a sense of wonder. It's a moment of pure enchantment, where time seems to pause.

40

# Insects

Celebrating the intricate beauty of the insect world, coloring pages showcase the diverse and fascinating creatures that inhabit our ecosystems, fostering appreciation for their unique characteristics.

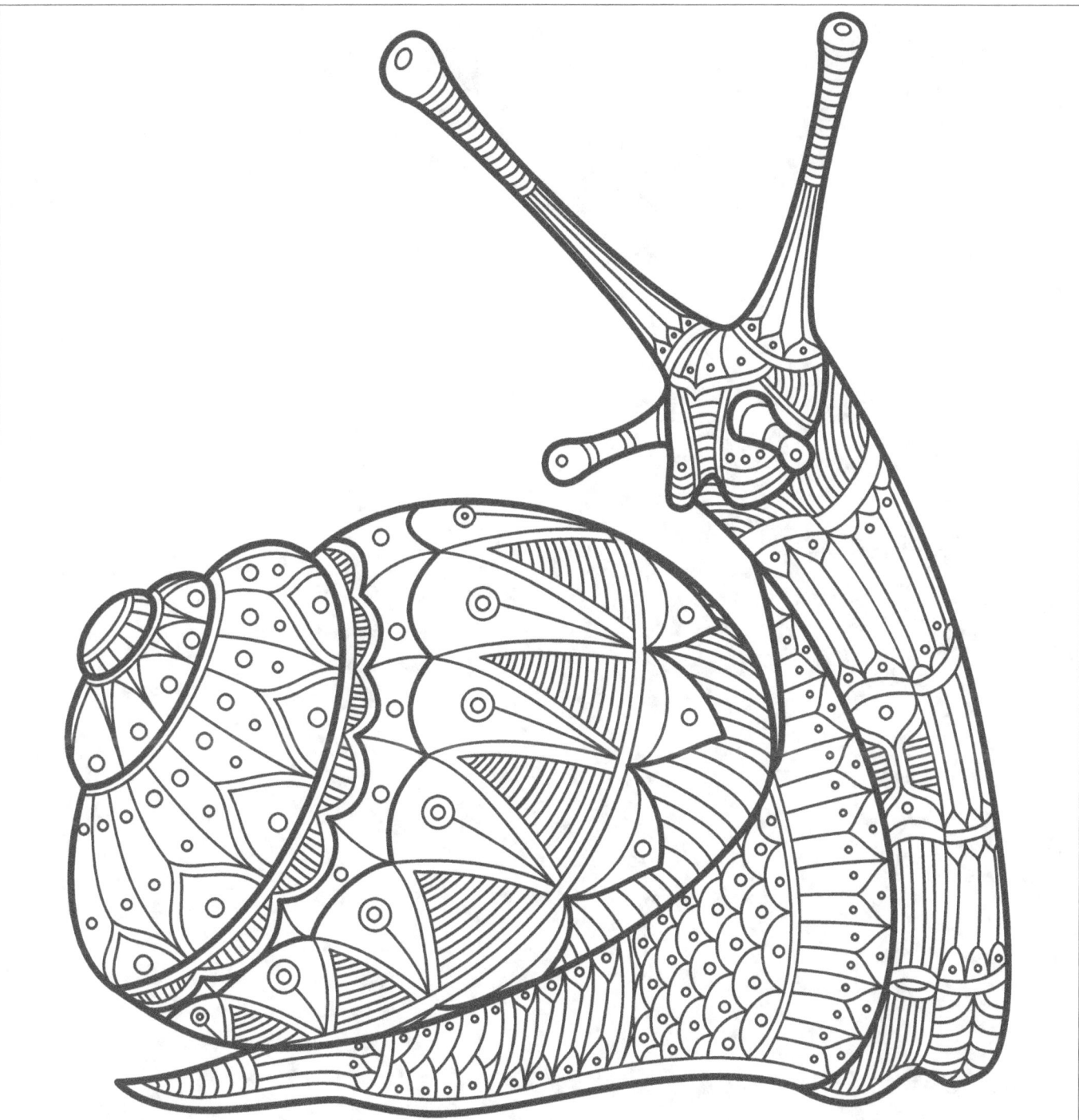

As the golden rays of the sun gently touch the horizon, begin your day with a series of sun salutations. Feel the warmth caress your skin and the earth beneath your feet. Take a deep breath, allowing the fresh morning air to invigorate your senses. With each flowing movement, embrace the stillness and serenity of the sunrise. Let the sun's radiant energy awaken your body and mind, filling you with a renewed sense of vitality. Embrace the beauty of this new day and let the sun salutations guide you towards a harmonious and balanced start.

**41**

# Moroccan Tile Designs

Drawing from Moroccan culture and craftsmanship, coloring pages highlight the mesmerizing patterns and vibrant colors of traditional tile designs, preserving and celebrating the artistry of this cultural heritage.

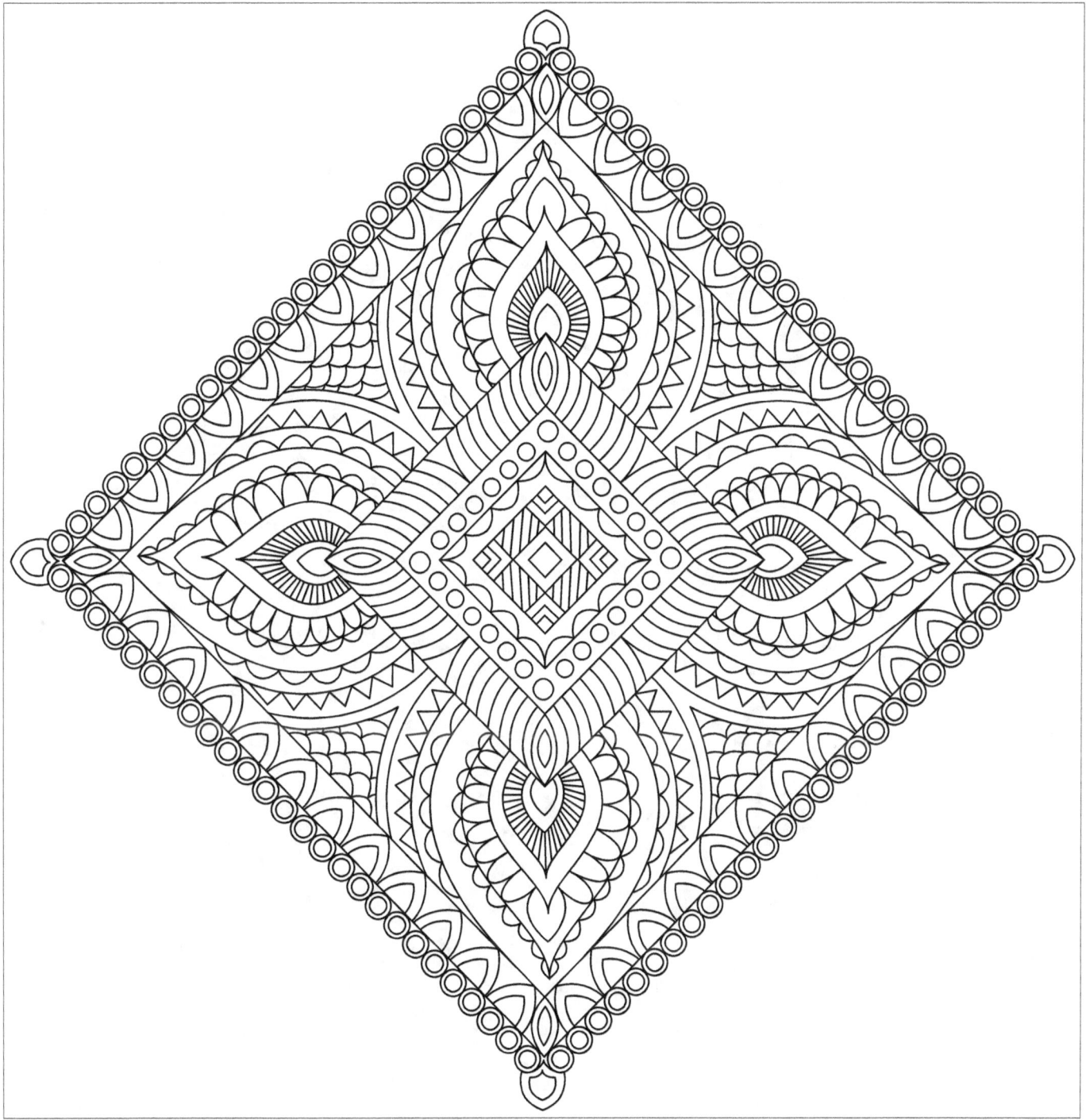

Look at the calm lake and see its peaceful reflection. The water is still, just like the quiet inside you. Stand by the quiet shore and think about the soft ripples and the gentle sounds of nature. Let your thoughts settle down like the calm water, and let go of any worries. Take a deep breath and feel the calming atmosphere around you. Let it bring you peace and clarity. In this moment of reflection, find comfort and embrace the deep stillness within you.

42

# Tribal Masks

Rooted in ancient rituals and traditions, coloring pages capture the essence of tribal masks, allowing individuals to explore the symbolism and cultural significance behind these captivating artifacts.

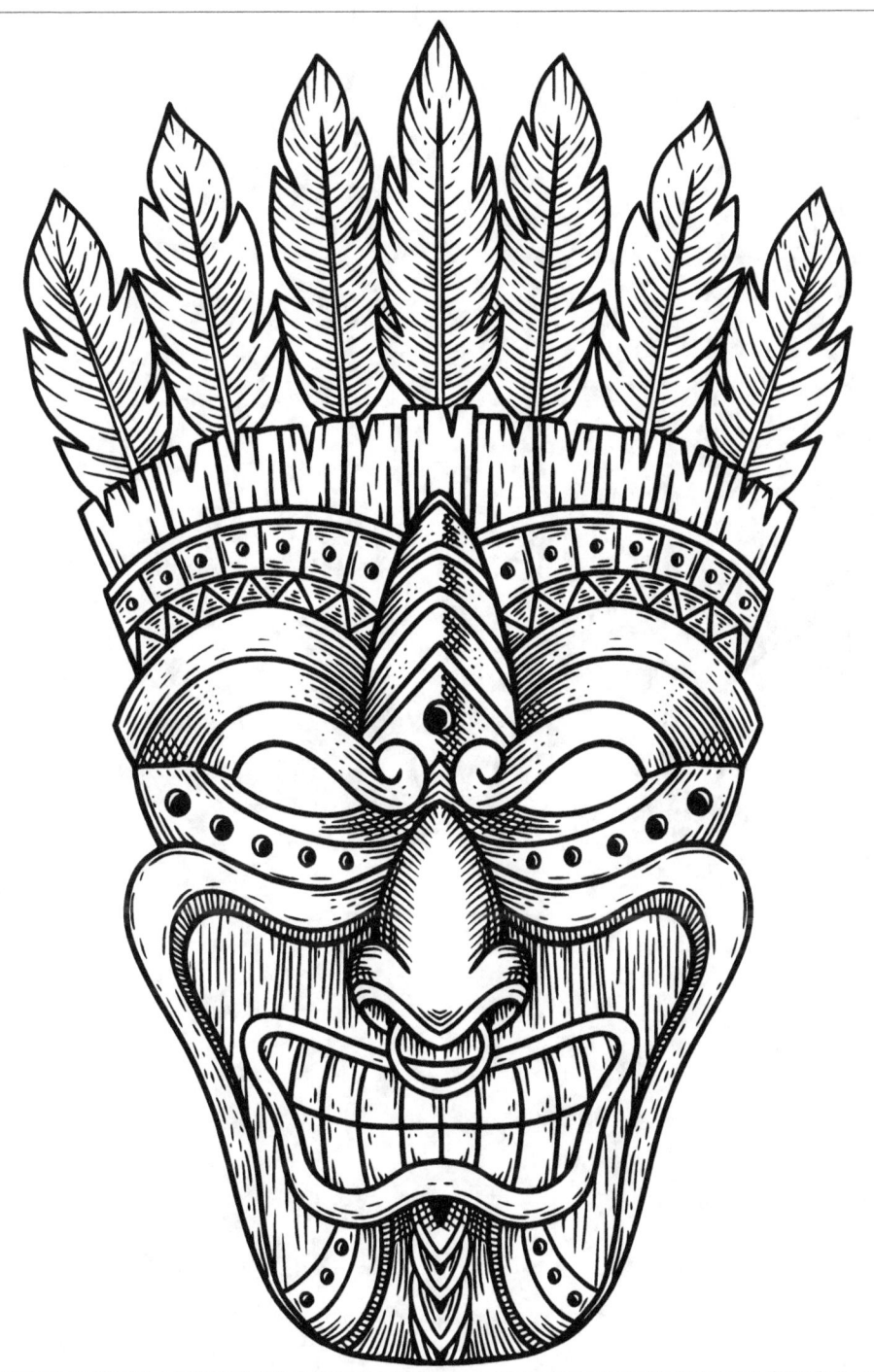

Focus your attention on the soothing sound of the meditation bell. Close your eyes and let yourself become fully present in this moment. Allow the sound to wash over you, bringing a sense of peace and stillness. Let go of any distractions and simply be here, fully aware of the present moment. The gentle chime of the bell guides your awareness, helping you stay centered and focused. Embrace the calmness that comes with this mindful practice and let the bell be your anchor in the present.

43

# Renaissance Portraits

Reflecting the artistic mastery of the Renaissance era, coloring pages feature portraits of prominent figures, offering a glimpse into the sophistication and elegance of this pivotal period in art history.

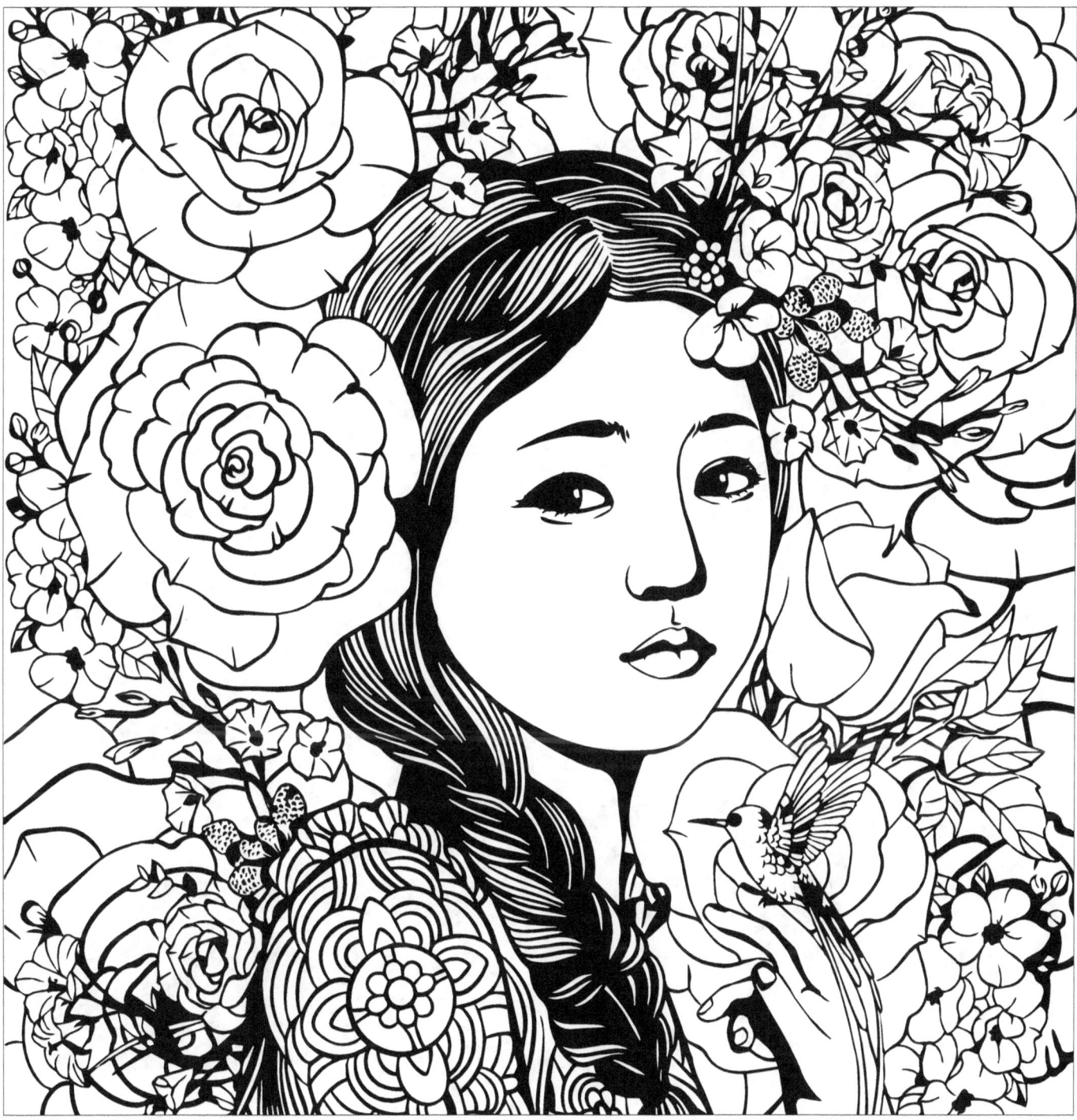

Imagine yourself standing in a vast rose farm, surrounded by rows of vibrant roses in full bloom. Inhale deeply, filling your lungs with the intoxicating scent of the flowers. Take a moment to appreciate the delicate beauty of each rose, their petals gently moving in the air. Find a comfortable spot to sit, perhaps under a shaded tree, and feel the soft grass beneath you. Allow yourself to be fully present in this serene environment, where the beauty of nature surrounds you.

44

# Indian Rangoli

Drawing inspiration from Indian traditions, coloring pages showcase the intricate and colorful patterns of Rangoli, celebrating the auspicious and vibrant art form.

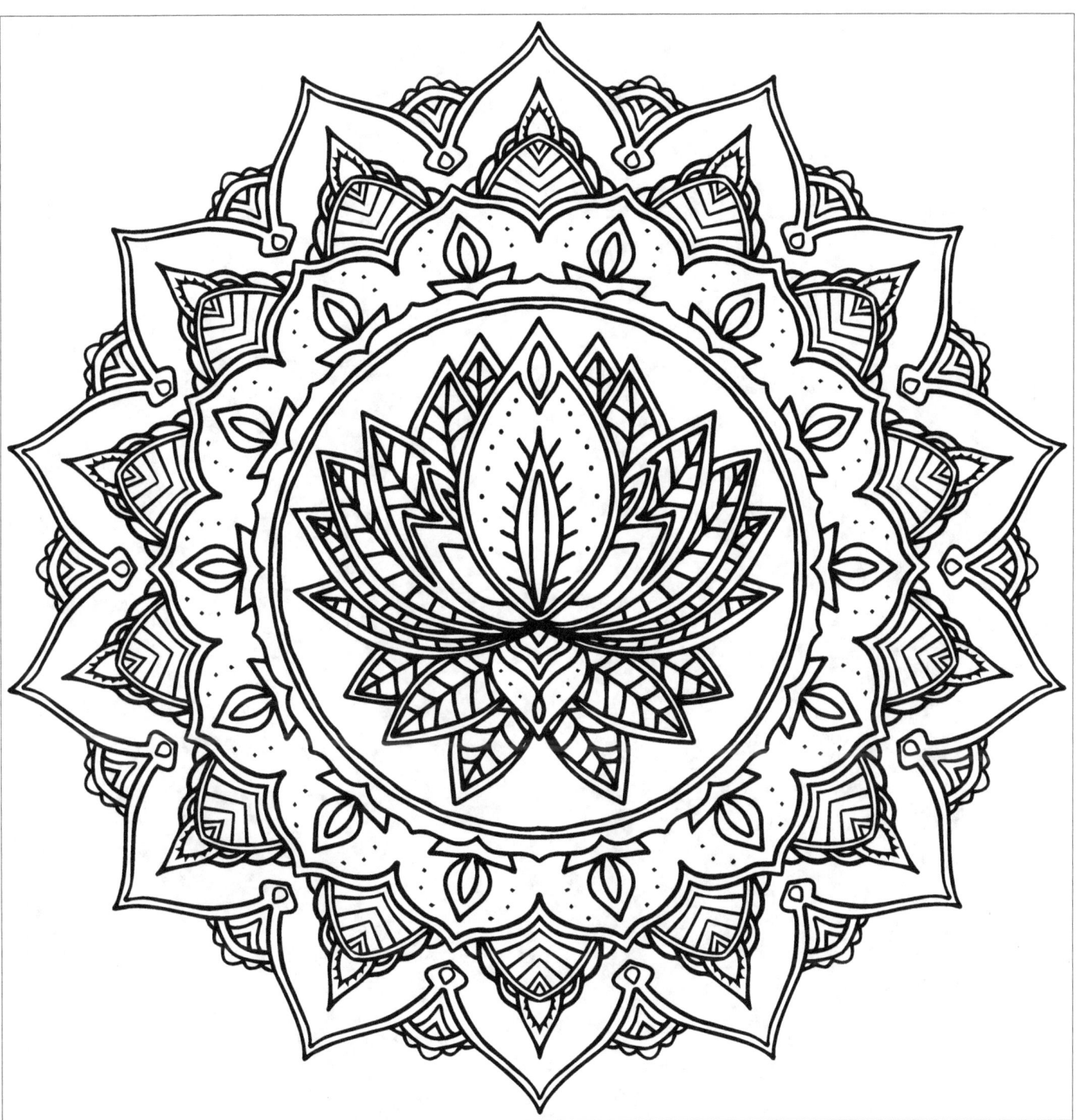

Close your eyes and imagine standing beneath a nurturing rain shower. Feel the gentle touch of raindrops on your skin, refreshing and invigorating you. Each drop carries with it a sense of renewal and cleansing. As the water cascades down, let it wash away any tension or worries, leaving you feeling revitalized and calm. Hear the rhythmic patter of raindrops on leaves and the soft whispers of nature surrounding you. Embrace this moment of peace and let the nourishing rain shower envelop you in its soothing embrace.

**45**

# Surrealistic Elements

Embracing the bizarre and unexpected, coloring pages with surrealistic elements challenge conventional reality, inviting colorists to unleash their creativity and explore unconventional artistic expressions.

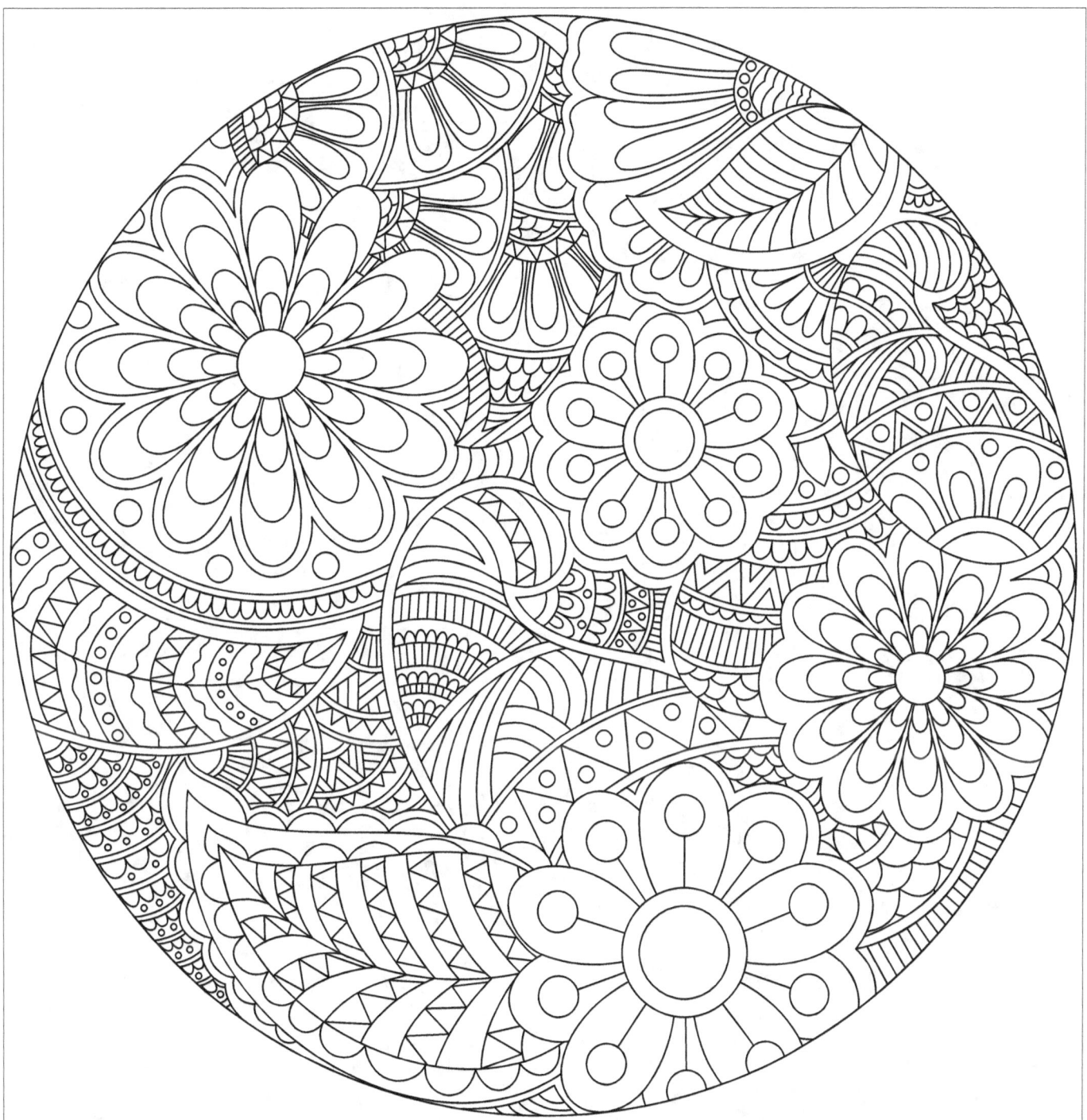

Imagine a serene morning on a secluded beach. The golden rays of the sun paint the sky in a beautiful display of colors. As you stroll along the smooth sand, it feels warm beneath your bare feet. The rhythmic waves gently kiss the shore, creating a symphony of soothing sounds. Inhale deeply and savor the invigorating scent of the salty sea air. Allow yourself to unwind and embrace the peace of this idyllic moment. Feel a sense of inner calm as you connect with the gentle rhythm of nature.

**46**

# Raptors

Honoring the power and majesty of birds of prey, coloring pages depict raptors in flight, capturing their grace and strength, allowing individuals to appreciate and connect with these magnificent creatures.

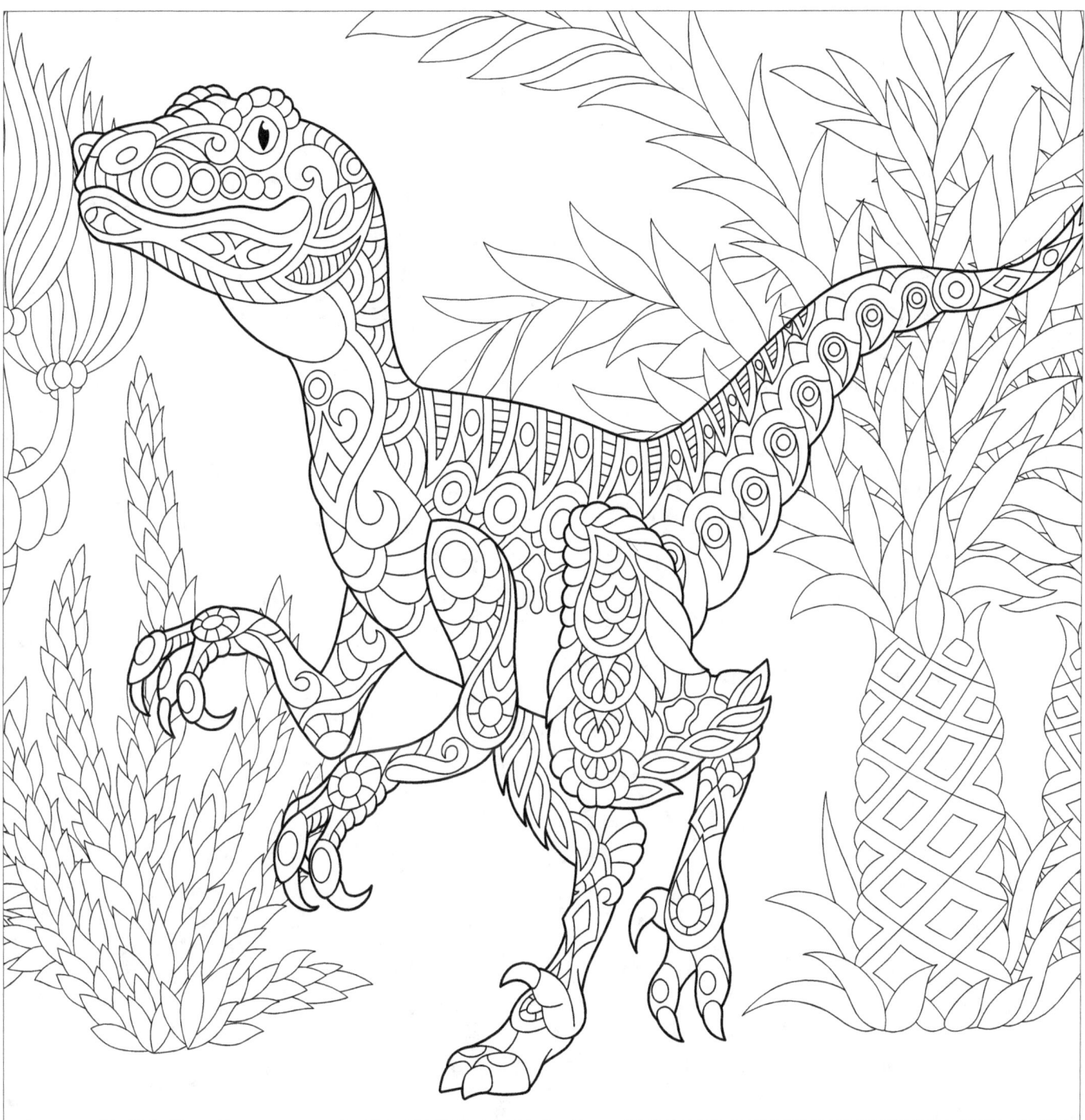

Experience a gentle yoga flow to relax and unwind. Find a comfy space and take a deep breath, releasing any tension. Start with easy stretches, moving smoothly between poses. Feel your muscles gently stretch as you move gracefully. Let your breath guide you, inhaling for relaxation and exhaling to let go of stress. Stay present, focusing on how your body feels. Let go of expectations and go with the flow. Each movement brings more relaxation and peace. End with a moment of stillness to absorb the benefits.

# Traditional Tea Houses

Drawing from cultural customs and traditions, coloring pages depict serene tea houses, inviting individuals to indulge in the tranquility and beauty of traditional tea ceremonies.

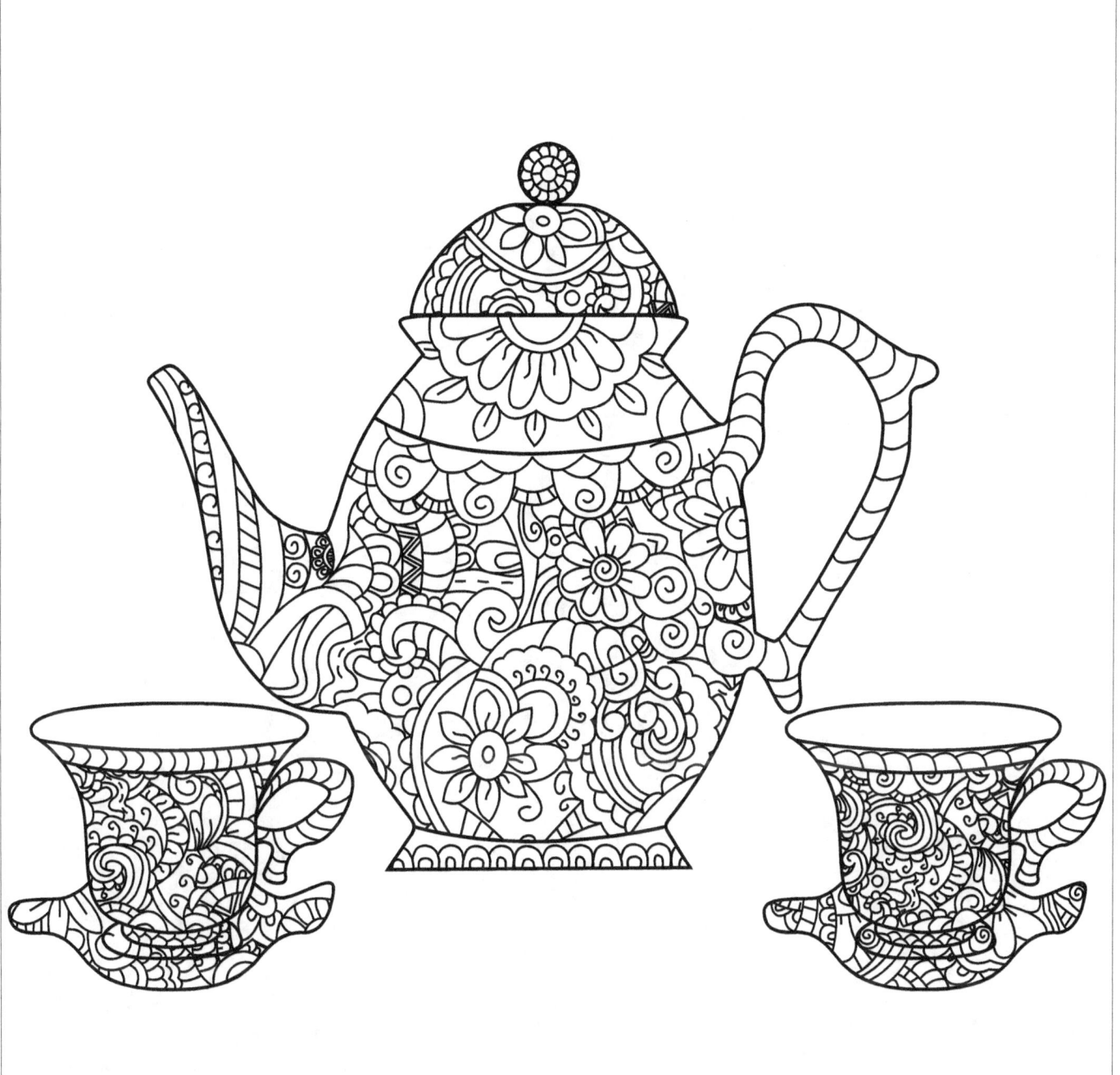

Experience the rejuvenating power of bathing in a peaceful forest. Find a quiet spot surrounded by nature's beauty. Fill a bathtub with warm water and natural scents. Submerge yourself in the soothing water, feeling the gentle caress on your skin. Close your eyes and listen to the sounds of the forest, the rustling of leaves and the chirping of birds. Let the serenity of the forest seep into your being, washing away stress and worry. Allow the healing energies of nature to envelop you, revitalizing your body and mind.

48

# Holidays

Originating from the joyous spirit of holiday celebrations, offer a creative outlet for individuals to immerse themselves in the festive atmosphere.

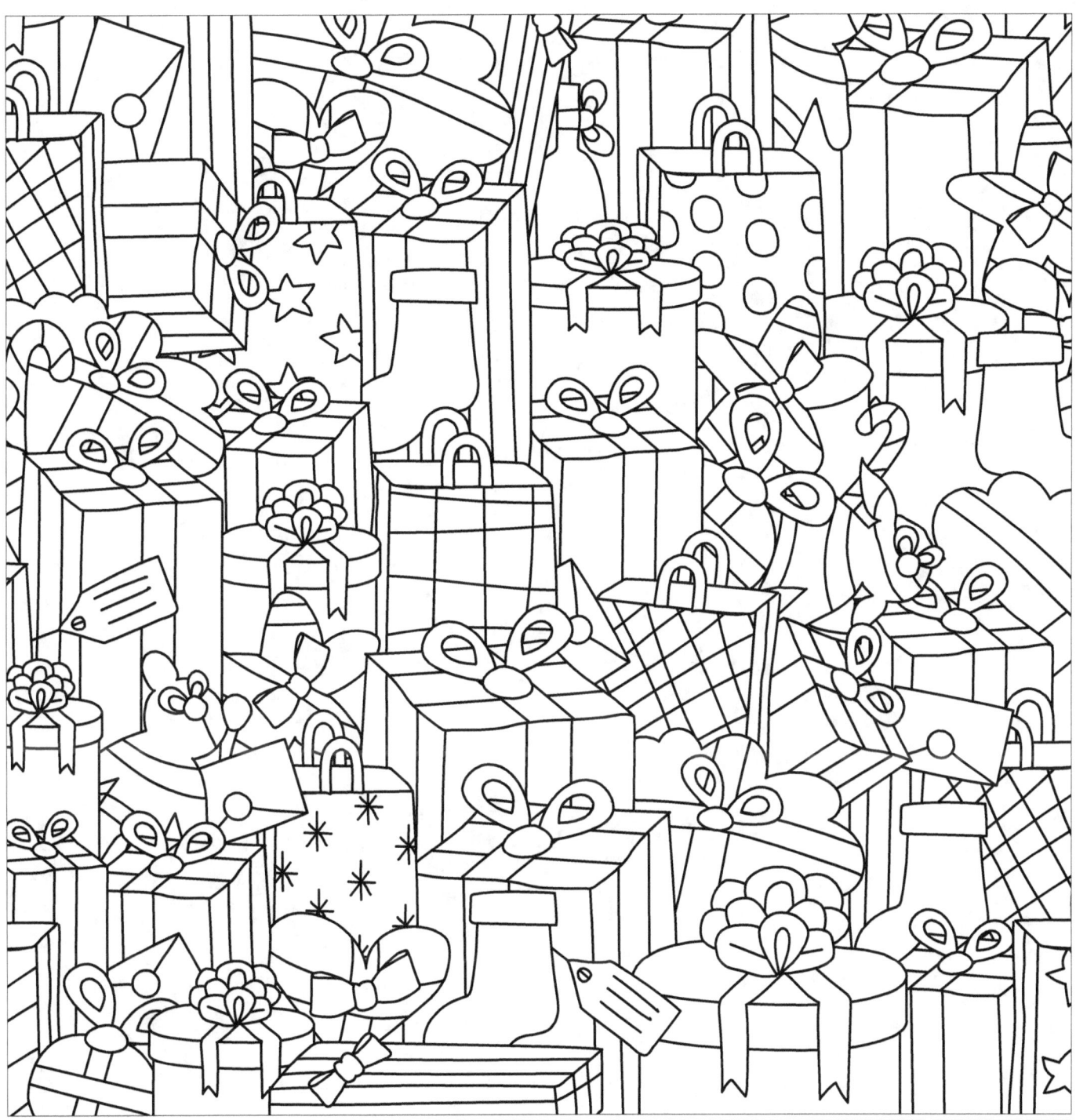

As the sun sets and darkness blankets the sky, find a quiet place to lie down and gaze at the night sky. Take a deep breath and let your body relax. Look up at the sparkling stars above, their shimmering lights filling the vast space. Feel the peacefulness of the night surrounding you, bringing a sense of calm. With each breath, release any thoughts or concerns, and be fully present in this moment of stargazing meditation. Sense a profound connection with the universe as you immerse yourself in the beauty and wonder of the night sky.

**49**

# Treasures

Treasures, reminiscent of cherished possessions and hidden gems, provide an enchanting escape for colorists, allowing you to unleash your imagination and bring life to intricate designs.

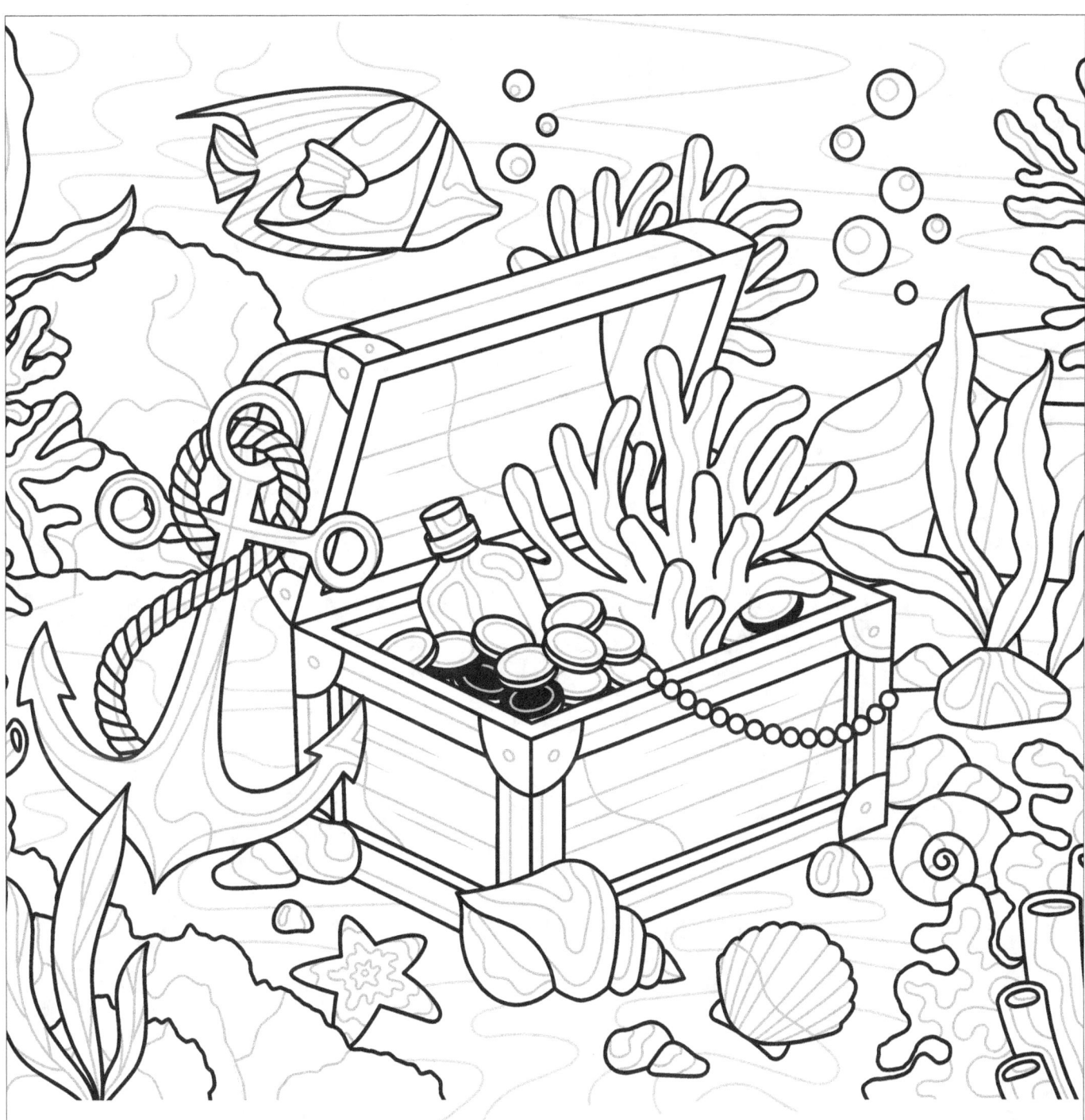

Imagine yourself seated on the moon, a place of serene solitude. With eyes closed, take a deep breath and let the stillness envelop you. The cosmic silence allows you to connect with the vastness of the universe. As you gaze at the distant stars, feel a sense of calm wash over you. The gentle hum of celestial energy fills the air, grounding you in this ethereal moment. Embrace the tranquility and surrender to the peacefulness that exists within and around you. Let the moonlight guide you on a journey of inner peace and harmony.

**50**

www.ingramcontent.com/pod-product-compliance
Lightning Source LLC
Chambersburg PA
CBHW080609220526
45466CB00010B/3292